'If you think a "manifesto" about Christianity must be something stern, abstract and doctrinaire, think again. Dave Tomlinson's heartfelt storytelling shows how Christian life unfolds in response to a God "as pervasive as the air about us, as universal as breathing." This is a generous and faithful book.'

Sara Miles, author of *Take This Bread* and *City of God*

'Like Jesus, Dave Tomlinson tells compelling stories from everyday life which re-frame both our idea of God and of what it means to be human. Be warned, these stories could change your life. Be reassured, it will be for the better . . . If this is what it means to be a bad Christian, sign me up.'

The Right Revd Clive Gregory, Bishop of Wolverhampton

'I confess: there are days when religion and its discontents get me down. But then Dave Tomlinson comes along and articulates a way of being faithful that puts a smile on my face, a song in my heart, a dance in my step, and hope in my heart. I'm grateful for *The Bad Christian's Manifesto*, and for the sagely and winsome insight of Dave Tomlinson.'

Brian D. McLaren, author of *We Make the Road by Walking*

'For all those bruised by life and demonised by the church, here is an oasis of sanity – a way of finding the bigger picture despite the sneering of small minds. This is the *Honest to God* for the twenty-first century.'

Mike Riddell, author of *The Insatiable Moon*

'Wherever you are on the scale of believer to non-believer, Dave has that rare ability to be abl⸱ ⸱ ⸱ book has something that we car religious perspective. Dave speak his often confusing world that we are accepted. And that is al

D1350897

Pippa Evans, comed Assembly

For my wife Pat,
whose voice and influence
is present throughout this book

The Bad Christian's Manifesto

Reinventing God
(and other modest proposals)

Dave Tomlinson

With illustrations by Rob Pepper

HODDER &
STOUGHTON

Unless indicated otherwise, Scripture quotations are taken from the
Holy Bible, New Revised Standard Version (Anglicised edition).
Copyright 1989 by the Division of Christian Education of the
National Council of the Churches of Christ in the USA. Used by permission.

First published in Great Britain in 2014 by Hodder & Stoughton
An Hachette UK company

1

Copyright © Dave Tomlinson, 2014
Illustrations copyright © Rob Pepper, 2014
'Sacrament' copyright © Martin Wroe, used by permission

The right of Dave Tomlinson to be identified as the Author of the Work has been
asserted by him in accordance with the Copyright, Designs and Patents Act 1988.

All rights reserved. No part of this publication may be reproduced, stored
in a retrieval system, or transmitted, in any form or by any means without
the prior written permission of the publisher, nor be otherwise circulated
in any form of binding or cover other than that in which it is published and
without a similar condition being imposed on the subsequent purchaser.

A CIP catalogue record for this title is available from the British Library

ISBN 9781444752250
eBook ISBN 9781444752267

Typeset in Sabon MT by Hewer Text UK Ltd, Edinburgh
Printed and bound in the UK by CPI Group (UK) Ltd, Croydon, CR0 4YY

Hodder & Stoughton policy is to use papers that are natural, renewable
and recyclable products and made from wood grown in sustainable
forests. The logging and manufacturing processes are expected to
conform to the environmental regulations of the country of origin.

Hodder & Stoughton Ltd
338 Euston Road
London NW1 3BH

www.hodderfaith.com

Contents

1. A tired old man upstairs
can I still believe in God?

Against some images of God the revolt of atheism is an act of pure religion.

Walter Wink

No one could forget Jim's funeral – the one where the Sex Pistols showed up instead of Frank Sinatra.

Despite a rainstorm of near biblical proportions, more than three hundred people arrived at the crematorium. Those who couldn't squeeze into the chapel peered through the open door from the entrance hall, some even stood outside in the rain listening to the service relayed from speakers.

Grief strikes hard when a person dies young, and at just thirty-five years, it felt like Jim's life had barely begun. When six of his friends carried his coffin into the chapel, the sobs and moans were so loud I could scarcely make myself heard. But little by little, the tears and groans morphed into smiles and laughter when one speaker after another related funny and moving accounts of Jim's short but eventful life.

The stories and tributes over, I invited the congregation to join me in commending Jim to God's loving care.

Nothing now remained but for me to hit the button to send Jim on his way. Glancing towards the chapel attendant, I nodded for the final track to commence.

That's when it happened. Bellowing through the speakers: the debauched, warbling sneer of Sid Vicious:

> *And n-o-o-o-w the end is n-e-e-e-ar,*
> *And so I fa-a-a-ce the final curt-ain.*
> *. . . Ha Ha Ha, . . .*

The entire gathering stood stock-still as the contemptuous obscenity in the next line of the song reverberated around the chapel. There was a pause; an intake of breath. Then, in one gloriously anarchic moment, every single soul erupted into rapturous applause and laughter. 'Jim, you crazy bugger!' one man shouted above the tumult, 'We love you!'

'WE LOVE YOU!' the congregation hollered back in unison, as if rehearsed.

Everybody laughed . . . and cried . . . and laughed . . . all the way to the pub.

Frank Sinatra's 'My way' is probably the nation's favourite funeral song but no one had requested the Sex Pistols' version – until Jim. I swear I heard him giggling in the background as the congregation stood open-mouthed.

Jim was HIV-positive and died of an AIDS-related illness. We met in the hospital where he spent his final months and where I served as the chaplain. Our many conversations on the ward focused mostly on music and football. Jim was allergic to religion. Which is why it surprised me when he asked if I would take his funeral.

I find it strange and slightly disconcerting to plan someone's funeral with the person sitting there in front of me, large as life. I never get used to that. But Jim eased the process with his dark humour and reassuring, down-to-earth manner.

When it came to discussing the final song he stuck to his guns despite a barrage of protests from his partner, Mario. 'It'll be a blast,' Jim said, grinning from ear to ear. 'I only wish I could be there to see their faces.'

'Yeah. That's the problem,' Mario piped up. 'I *will* be there!'

We laughed, like three mates sharing a joke in the bar after work.

Just before leaving, I reached across the bed to give Jim a hug. He recoiled sharply, exclaiming: 'No, Dave! Don't touch me. Don't touch me. I'm unclean.'

'Unclean?' I said. 'What on earth are you talking about, unclean?'

It turned out that in his early teens Jim attended a church with tub-thumping sermons about the 'abomination' of homosexuality. He knew he was gay from a young age but never told anyone until he confessed to the vicar. After that he became engulfed in weeks of so-called 'counselling' which was actually nothing short of emotional abuse. Week-in, week-out, the vicar attempted to 'deliver' Jim from a 'spirit of homosexuality'. A confused teenager, he went along with it, trying his best to change, to become 'normal'.

But surprise, surprise, it all came to nothing – Jim still fancied boys, not girls! So he ditched church and religion,

4

came out to his friends and family, and got on with his life as a young gay man. Years later, after contracting the HIV virus, he met Mario. They fell madly in love and lived happily together for ten years prior to his death.

Yet despite turning his back on religion, Jim never quite managed to root out the shame embedded in his teenage psyche. And when I went to hug him, it all burst forth. 'The last time a man of the cloth put his arm around me,' he said, 'it was to tell me "lovingly" that I would go to hell if I didn't stop looking at boys.'

Jim paused. Winced. Then said, 'But what if he was right, Dave? What if the "man upstairs" really doesn't like gays . . . people like me? What if—'

'Okay. Stop right there, Jim,' I interrupted. 'Let's get this clear: being gay is *not* a sin. It's in the same category as being left-handed, or having red hair, or being a boy instead of a girl. You can't help it. It's normal. No one chooses to be gay, it's just who you are – right?'

'Right,' he echoed.

'Trust me, Jim, you were misled. God loves you just as you are: a beautiful gay man. You have your flaws like the rest of us, but being gay isn't one of them.'

We hugged – and wept. Actually, Jim turned out to be one of the best huggers I have known. We embraced many times in the weeks that followed. And yes, I did manage to convince him that 'God likes fags', as he cheekily enjoyed putting it; that God liked him!

I have a basically sunny disposition. I don't rile easily. But what truly gets my goat is misery inflicted in the name of God. On the way home I pulled the car over, too angry to cry, though I wanted to. Sitting there at the side of the road in silent indignation I contemplated what sort of God makes a man feel unclean for loving another man with all the passion, tenderness and commitment I feel towards my wife? No God that I can recognise, or want anything to do with. That's for sure!

There and then, I resolved to be an atheist in the face of any God or religion that torments the likes of Jim, or that increases rather than diminishes the sum of human misery. If God exists, she or he has to be better than this.

In my earlier days as a Christian it all seemed so straightforward. When someone asked if I believed in God, I could respond confidently. Yes, of course I believed in God. But now it feels more complicated. It really depends on which God you have in mind.

I don't believe in an old white man with a beard, sitting in the heavens.

I don't believe in a God who treats gay people as deviants or as unclean.

I don't believe in a God who inspires vengeance and war, or incites bigotry and sectarianism.

I don't believe in a God who consigns people to everlasting torment for not 'accepting' Jesus.

I don't believe in a God who presides over the world like some 'fat controller' deciding where and when to intervene in human affairs.

I don't believe in a God who has some absolute 'plan' or 'design' for our lives and for the world to which we are supposed to conform, or else.

So what sort of God *do* I believe in? This is what I hope to reveal in the rest of this book: not with philosophical and theological arguments (though there will be plenty of them tucked away in the background), or by simply quoting creeds and Christian dogma, but mostly by looking at how we *experience* God in our lives and in the world. And trust me, we do all experience God in some way or other, by whatever name.

Naturally, most people associate God with religion, but I have to say that if I were in charge of God's public relations, I would definitely see this as a mixed blessing. I might even be tempted to tell the press, 'God doesn't do religion!' A religious God is too small, too narrow, too sectarian. God is either the God of the entire world, of all people – religious and non-religious – or not at all. And, in fact, the experience of God is the most democratic phenomenon imaginable: as pervasive as the air about us, as universal as breathing. Yet like the air about us, like the act of breathing, we are mostly unaware of it.

What I am proposing in this book is that God is not alien to any one of us, religious or not; that there are things identifiable in the experience of all of us to which the name 'God' might refer.

Yet the fact remains that for some people the very word 'God' is so contaminated by bad experiences and negative perceptions of religion that it is no longer usable. I have a close friend who describes himself as an atheist. I'm not sure that he is, but he certainly has no stomach for religion or for the God it portrays. He is not alone. Millions of people feel alienated by religious beliefs and practices or by their experiences of churches and church people. And sadly, God gets lumped together with this.

In her intriguing song 'Him', the pop singer Lily Allen ponders how God may feel about the cruelty and abuse carried out in his name. Teasingly, she wonders if he's skint or financially secure, and when it comes to election time, who he'd vote for. He certainly wouldn't ever feel suicidal – his favourite band is Creedence Clearwater Revival. But despite her typical playfulness, the singer poignantly laments that ever since he can remember people have died in his good name.

I grew up thinking that blaspheming, 'taking God's name in vain', meant shouting profanities such as 'God almighty!' or 'Jesus Christ!' I now think that many so-called profanities are in fact unintentional prayers, and that the real blasphemy is the pain we inflict on people in the name of God, or when we write off whole swathes of humanity because they don't believe what we believe about God, or use the same religious jargon.

The great Jewish philosopher Martin Buber once proposed a freeze on the use of the word 'God'. Not because he didn't believe in God, but because he thought the word was often used in meaningless and even dangerous ways. A ban on 'God' isn't possible, of course, but it is worth pondering the prospect. After all, 'God' is just a word – a word that sometimes maligns or slanders the reality to which it seeks to refer. Who knows, perhaps an abstention from God-talk could even lead to a new and better understanding of who or what God is.

Blaise Pascal famously spoke of a God-shaped hole in the human heart – a sense of longing and incompleteness that only God can fill. If that void still exists (and I am sure it does), I fear that the God of organised religion may no longer be adequate to the task. We need a different God, a different vision of God that grips the hearts and minds of people in the twenty-first century.

In a fascinating conversation following a recent wedding, a marketing executive told me bluntly, 'the God "brand" needs reinventing. The world has changed, religion is out of fashion, and God feels irrelevant.' I think he has a point.

Last year I went on a radio show just before Christmas to discuss why it is that lots of people suddenly turn up at church for Midnight Mass or Christmas morning. 'Doesn't it annoy you that they stay away all year, then just roll up when it suits them?' the presenter asked me.

'Maybe that's the only time that we have something on offer which they really want,' I replied. 'If I opened a shop on the high street and nobody came in to buy my products, it would be a bit rich to blame the customers for not turning up. I'm not saying that religion is a product to market and sell, but if the church isn't in some way meeting a demand or a perceived need, there is no point in moaning when people don't turn up.'

There is an old religious joke about a man who fell off the edge of a cliff but managed to grab the branch of a tree growing out of the side of the rock. Hanging on for dear life, the man yelled 'Help! Is there anybody up there?' A voice came back, 'Yes, this is God, and I can help you. But you must trust me. Just let go of the branch and I will save you. All will be well.' There was a short pause. The man wriggled his hands to get a better grip, and then shouted, 'Is there anybody *else* up there?'

Most people today are not greatly antagonistic towards the notion of God; militant atheism remains a small minority interest. But many have lost confidence that the voice of God in religion has much useful to say. God has become like a tired old man in the background, to be ignored.

Yet there is plenty of spiritual hunger about. Lots of people are hanging on to branches, desperately hoping for a helping hand. It's a matter of credibility. In ancient times it seemed reasonable for a 'man upstairs' type of God to rule the world from the top floor in a triple-decker universe, but this God no longer translates in a post-Newtonian, a post-Darwinian, and a post-feminist world. The idea of a male God, a kingly figure 'out there' ruling the universe, randomly intervening from time to time, now appears silly and untenable to most people. If religion is to continue to make sense we need some different notion of divinity that engages with the circumstances, needs and sensibilities of the twenty-first century.

But the truth is, we have always reinvented God in the light of social, cultural and intellectual developments. 'God' evolves with time, or at least, the image and notion of God we hold in our psyche evolves, and it is this process of evolution that enables us to experience God in fresh ways, appropriate to changing circumstances and shifting sensibilities.

At a pastoral level, I help people to reinvent God all the time: to ditch internalised images of God that cause suffering and self-recrimination, and to discover a God of unconditional love, who enables them to flourish and be the people they deep down wish to be.

Jim is a wonderful example of someone whose notion and experience of God was reinvented. Sadly, it occurred just months before he died. Yet the pleasure of knowing that he could finally look deep into his own soul and know that the person he saw was loved and accepted by God will live with me forever.

This book is a manifesto for change – not in the sense of offering a programme or master plan, more like notes on the back of a (quite large) envelope. If you are content with your notion of God and of religion (as a believer or a sceptic), or if you feel you have the meaning of life sorted, this book may not be for you.

I write for the discontented, for fellow strugglers – bad Christians/Muslims/Jews/Buddhists/Hindus/pagans/ agnostics/atheists – who sense that, perhaps, beyond their doubts and questions, beyond their discontent, stands a mystery worth exploring, which some of us call God.

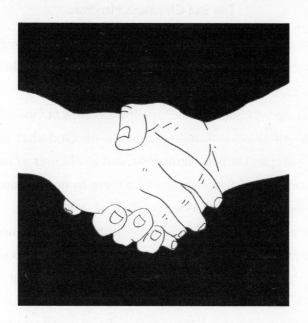

2. Bad Christian meets good atheist

arguments about religion are boring

Only an atheist can be a good Christian; only a Christian can be a good atheist.

Ernst Bloch

It's Sunday morning, 11am.

The once grand but now dilapidated Victorian church in North London is packed to the rafters: every seat taken, every inch of standing room occupied. Volunteers bunch the chairs closer together, adding benches and children's seats wherever possible to squeeze a few more bodies in. But that's it. No space left. The doors are closed. Dozens of latecomers are turned away.

It's a vicar's dream!

But there is no vicar.

This is no ordinary church service.

The background music from the live band dies down; a hush descends on the congregation. Then a lanky, bearded figure with long gingery hair, a huge grin and booming voice bounds onto the stage and grabs the microphone:

'WOW!

HELLO EVERYONE!

WELCOME TO THE SUNDAY ASSEMBLY!'

If Sanderson Jones looks and sounds more like a stand-up comic than a priest, it's because that is what he is – a stand-up comic. And together with his co-conspirator and fellow comedian, Pippa Evans, he created the Sunday Assembly, a 'godless congregation', described as 'part atheist church, part foot-stomping show, and one hundred per cent celebration of life'.

Godless, the Sunday Assembly may be, but any regular churchgoer who stumbles in by mistake will find much that is familiar. The service follows the time-honoured hymn-sandwich format – but without the hymns, which are replaced with pop songs like 'Don't stop me now' by Queen, and Bonnie Tyler's 'I'm holding out for a hero'. Pippa Evans and the band lead the singing, with the enthusiastic congregation following the lyrics on a large screen.

The service also features a reading, a sermon of sorts, some reflective silence that looks remarkably like prayer, and the obligatory collection to cover costs, during which people are encouraged to greet those sitting around them. Afterwards, people stay for a nice cup of tea and a biscuit.

The idea for the Sunday Assembly emerged from Jones's comedy gigs, where he encouraged his audiences to get to know one another, and they in turn pressed him for ways to stay in touch and even build small groups. There was clearly a hunger for community, he decided, and perhaps others would feel, as he did, that words like 'awe' and 'transcendence' should not be the preserve only of religion. 'So why not a church for the godless? After all, atheists have got just as much right to meet up, sing a few songs, and have a cup of tea with a stranger,' Sanderson reflects.

The idea struck a chord. Within months of its launch the Sunday Assembly grew to 600 regular attenders, with hundreds of requests pouring in for congregations to be rolled out in cities across the world. Not everyone who attends is 'godless'. Being atheist is not obligatory. Many are simply not religious; some are even churchgoers who prefer this to regular church.

Not long after the Assembly was launched, I met Sanderson for coffee, introduced by a mutual friend. We instantly hit it off. I loved his big personality, his infectious laughter which made the whole coffee shop turn around to see what was going on, and the twinkle in his eye which said he didn't take himself too seriously.

I also quickly sensed that Sanderson was no ideologue. His brand of 'not God', as he likes to call it, has little in common with the dogmatic, evangelical atheism of a Richard Dawkins. After reading my book *How to be a Bad Christian . . . and a Better Human Being*, Sanderson commented that my approach to Christianity was similar to his towards atheism. By which, I think he meant that neither of us is a fundamentalist – someone who deals in black and white certainties, with no shades of grey. Sanderson actually says that he thinks atheism is boring – 'Why are we defining ourselves by something we don't believe in?'

With a rapidly burgeoning congregation, and a shed-load of previously unthought-of questions to grapple with, Sanderson was eager to pick my brains, to learn some tricks of the 'trade'. We laughed at the irony of it all, especially when he recommended my book to an inquisitive waiter who browsed the copy sitting in front of us: 'You should read it. It's very good,' the waiter was told.

A couple of months later, I was invited to give a 'sermon' at the Sunday Assembly's Easter service. Easter and atheist are words most of us would not normally place in the same sentence, but Sanderson and Pippa thrive on intriguing contradictions.

I felt honoured to give a talk at the Sunday Assembly. Not many vicars get asked to speak at an atheist 'church'. I also relished the topic I was given: 'The power of stories, myths and metaphors as ways of seeing the world – and why Easter remains a compelling story.'*

Philip Pullman states that after nourishment, shelter and companionship, stories are the thing we need most in the world. I think he is right. Stories nourish the imagination. They enrich life on so many levels. They also play a massive part in the way we make sense of the world – religious stories, in particular.

But do our stories have to be true in order to give a true picture of things? Is fact and literal truth the only kind of

---

* See Appendix for the text of the sermon.

17

truth that counts? This was the question I addressed in my talk.

Very often, when people suspect that I'm a woolly liberal instead of a proper Christian they test my orthodoxy with questions about the virgin birth and the bodily resurrection of Christ. Don't get me wrong, I love a good argument; I can happily debate the finer points of theology until the cows come home (and often do, my wife tells me!). But these questions are mostly predicated on the assumption that we have to be one kind of literalist or another: either a religious literalist who equates truth with fact, or a scientific literalist who also equates truth with fact but from the reverse standpoint.

The religious literalist assumes that a story cannot be true *unless* it is factual; the scientific literalist argues that *because* religious stories are not factual, they obviously cannot be true. I am not a literalist of either variety. I dislike all kinds of fundamentalism – religious and secular. But I do believe in truth, which is ultimately greater than facts and literal explanations. Anybody who loves art and music, or appreciates poetry and literature, knows that truth and fact do not necessarily add up to the same thing. I heard about a Native American Indian storyteller who prefaced his account of his tribe's creation myth with, 'I don't know if it really happened this way, but I know that this story is true.'

I have preached in many churches, addressed many Christian events around the world, but I don't believe I have experienced a more receptive audience than the Sunday Assembly, which convinces me that a far more constructive engagement can occur between atheists and people of faith than we have witnessed in recent times. Perhaps the Sunday Assembly represents a shift towards post-New Atheism,[*] a more mellow, less dogmatic position, which, as Sanderson says, feels less driven to define itself by what it doesn't believe. The motto of the Sunday Assembly is 'Live better, help often, wonder more.' Who cannot subscribe to that?

The starting point for a more positive engagement is the assumption that we are fundamentally looking for the same things, though pursuing them in different ways, under different headings. So far as I can tell, Pippa, Sanderson and their atheist friends in the Sunday Assembly are looking for truth and meaning with similar fervour and openness to me and my Christian friends.

---

[*] 'New Atheism' is the name given to the ideas promoted by a collection of modern atheists like Richard Dawkins, Daniel Dennett, Sam Harris and Christopher Hitchens – the so-called 'Four Horsemen' of New Atheism.

They too hope for a more just and compassionate world; they too try to make good choices in life; they too feel grateful to be alive in a wondrous universe; they too are looking for ways to enrich their lives and those of others; they too value honesty and integrity. But for whatever reasons they find the word 'God' just doesn't work for them.

Arguing about God and religion can become very tedious. However, looking for common ground, for ways to collude in the cause of love, peace and justice in the world – that gets very exciting.

When Sanderson and I met in the coffee shop, there were no labels, no 'Christian' and 'atheist', just two people who soon discovered that they liked each other and became friends. Equally, when I stood to address the Sunday Assembly I didn't look out at an 'atheist' congregation needing to be converted, but at a gathering of human beings – friends and fellow travellers – meeting to deepen their experience of life, and to become better citizens of the world.

The problem with words like 'Christian' and 'atheist' is that they become categories to slot people into without discovering anything about the people themselves. Personally, I don't really care what label a person wears, I want to know about that person: what motivates them and why, what are their passions and longings, where have they come from on their journey, and where would they like to be?

After my talk at the Sunday Assembly, I joined the throng of 'godless' who piled into a nearby pub – debating God and 'not-God' is thirsty business! Before long a group huddled around me, asking questions about my talk.

'I was surprised – and a little disturbed – at how much I liked what you said,' Jonny confessed, sipping on his beer. 'It tempted me to check out church again. Trouble is, when I hear Christians talk about God I mostly cringe. It's like God is their mate, or something. I find it really embarrassing.'

I agreed. I too find religious God-talk awkward and uncomfortable at times.

'But do you really think God exists?' Michelle asked.

'What *is* God?' someone else piped up.

'I think God is a security blanket for people who can't cope,' another person chipped in.

Still quite sober, and reasonably lucid, I owned up to being an ontological realist but an epistemological relativist! In plain English: I do believe that 'God' refers to an actual reality, but I don't think that we have words, categories or explanations to describe who or what that reality is.

Basically, 'existence' isn't a good way to think of God. Paul Tillich, one of the twentieth century's greatest Christian thinkers, made the shrewd observation that if when we think of the word 'God' we are thinking of a reality that may or may not exist, we are not thinking of God. So 'existence' is too limited a category. God isn't a being among other beings – not even the Supreme Being – God is the 'ground of being', or 'being itself'.

However, it is important to acknowledge that the notion of God was not invented by academics dreaming up complicated ideas and theories. It arose from ordinary people sensing that there is something beyond the world of visible things. Or as I would prefer to put it, that there is a 'beyond' *within* the world of visible things, a hidden depth to life and the universe, which I call 'God'.

In the normal course of events, most of our life continues on the surface. We are caught up with the routines of daily life in work and pleasure, seldom stopping to look to the heights above or to the depths beneath. Then, when some sort of earthquake occurs – a bereavement, a relationship breakdown, some sort of disappointment, an experience of great joy, a sudden burst of curiosity – the surface is broken and we realise that there is a great dimension of depth to life. Then we start to delve deeper, to enquire about the meaning of things.

Actually, life is full of nudges and prompts to look deeper, but mostly they go unnoticed or unheeded. Every part of life summons us to explore its hidden qualities: a beautiful urban tree at the side of a busy road, an intriguing graffiti image, a distant church bell, the colourful melancholy of an autumn walk, a vague whiff that transports you to another time or place – all these things and more beckon us to comb beyond the surface of life, to reach towards the depth of being itself.

Once we begin the inner journey, we find that it is like peeling an onion, but the onion grows bigger rather than smaller as each layer is removed. However deeply we delve into life's mysteries there is always more to explore, more to discover. The depths are infinite and inexhaustible. And the name of this infinite and inexhaustible depth to life is 'God', the ground of all being, existence itself.

Paul Tillich argues that once we understand that depth is what the word 'God' means, we cannot truly claim to be an atheist. Within this frame of reference, the true atheist would be the person who insists that life has no depth, that life is shallow and empty. Anyone who understands anything about depth knows much about God. And as Tillich says, if the word 'God' has not much meaning for you, translate it, and speak of the depths of your life, of the source of your being, of your ultimate concern, of what you take seriously without any reservation.

It seems to me that it is time to stop bickering over theology, to stop hurling brickbats at each other, and discover a deeper unity within our common humanity. Ultimately, it is not doctrines or propositions that unite (or divide) us but the level of our commitment to journey into the depths of life – whether Christian, Muslim, Buddhist, atheist or whatever.

Ideally, religion should help us on this journey, but sometimes it doesn't; sometimes it stands in the way. And ironically (considering I am a vicar), I sometimes advise people to give up religion, at least for a while, for their mental health's sake: to stop reading the Bible, praying and going to church, because the vision of God created or reinforced by this religious activity is destroying them, psychologically and emotionally.

Brenda is a good example of this. She grew up in a staunchly Christian home, controlled by her obsessively religious father. She attended church, prayed, and read her Bible dutifully from childhood, yet the 'God' she internalised from these activities almost wrecked her life. Under the shadow of a horribly disapproving dad, who criticised her mercilessly, the 'heavenly father' she came to know turned out to be a larger-than-life expression of him, her contemptible earthly father.

24

When I met Brenda, in her mid-thirties, she had almost no self-esteem despite being a bright and beautiful woman with a successful career. She could recite verses from the Bible and utter religious platitudes about God's love, but in her heart she believed that God disapproved of virtually everything about her. 'God may love me,' she declared, 'but he definitely doesn't like me.' 'God' made Brenda's life a misery. 'I often think about committing suicide,' she told me, 'but I'm frightened I'll go to hell.'

She looked disconcerted when I suggested she should stop reading the Bible and praying, and seek therapy instead. But after six months of no church, no Bible and no prayer – and the help of a good therapist – she wrote me an email which read,

> When you told me to stop practising my faith I was devastated, outraged. I wasn't sure that I should trust you. You snatched away my security blanket. But everything is falling into place now. I was clinging to the thing that hurt me most . . . I'm starting to believe that instead of being angry at my failure, God may have actually grieved at my upbringing. His anger may have been directed at my father and the church rather than me . . . Perhaps God likes me after all.

At a later meeting, I asked Brenda if there was anyone who she felt had really loved her. 'My grandma!' she replied enthusiastically, a broad grin sweeping across her face.

'What is it about your grandma that makes you so happy?' I asked.

She proceeded to tell me how when she was a small child at her grandma's home she knocked over a treasured vase, a family heirloom. Knowing how important the vase was, the little girl screamed as it crashed to the ground. But when her grandma rushed into the room there was no anger, no recrimination, just relief. 'Thank God! I thought you were hurt' the old lady exclaimed, gathering Brenda into her arms. Recalling the story with teary eyes, Brenda announced, with a sense of self-worth which I hadn't seen in her before: 'And *that* was the day I discovered that *I* was my grandma's family treasure.'

'Brenda,' I said, looking her straight in the eye, 'what if God is like your grandma, not your dad? How would it change things if you imagined God as a warm motherly figure who gathers you into her arms when you do something wrong instead of the harsh father-figure who admonishes you?'

Brenda paused while the idea percolated through.

'Can I really picture my gran when I think about God?' she asked.

'Why not?' I said.

Reinventing God, or at least, reinventing the image and notion of God etched in her psyche, transformed Brenda's life for the better. She dumped the idea that God in any way resembled her father, and then began to flourish with a sense of inner acceptance.

So is God like Brenda's grandma? Well, yes . . . but . . . God is a mystery beyond all our imagining; no representation of God can be taken literally. So of course God is not literally like Brenda's grandma. Yet it is impossible to exaggerate the difference it made for Brenda to reinvent God – to begin to see God through the lens of her grandma's love.

So how can we hold these things together: the acknowledgement that God transcends all human categories, and our need for images of the divine which are powerful and liberating and humanly comprehensible? Hopefully, we will make a little more sense of this in the next chapter.

3. 'For one thing, she's black'
what does God really look like?

What comes into our minds when we think of God is the most important thing about us.

A.W. Tozer

The flight from London to St Louis took nine hours. It was 2am by the time I cleared immigration and found my hotel room. I sat up in bed wide awake, flicking through the TV channels, searching for something to occupy my jet-lagged brain.

Eventually I settled on one of the God channels, the sort my wife scorns me for watching. But, hey, she wasn't there; I could do what I liked. The show featured a man talking about a near-death experience (he called it his 'resurrection' experience). He told how, after leaving his body, he travelled through a tunnel of light and arrived in heaven where an angel greeted him and escorted him into the 'throne room' of God for a personal audience with the Almighty.

'How did God communicate with you?' the presenter enquired sincerely.

'He spoke to me in English,' the man said. Then, without batting an eyelid, added, 'with a Jewish New York accent!'

I literally fell off the bed, laughing uncontrollably.

I'm not sure what tickled me most: the deadpan-ness of the man as he shared his revelation, the wide-eyed credulity of the presenter who softly responded 'Wow!', or the utterly stunning idea that God sounds like Woody Allen.

At any rate, ever since that night one of my more cherished visions of God is of a tiny Woody Allen figure perched on a massive throne, wistfully muttering, 'The only thing standing between me and greatness is me.'

But how do *you* picture God? What sort of image comes to mind when you hear the name God mentioned?

How do you picture God if you close your eyes to pray? Is your God black or white, male or female, a person, a shape, a colour, a thing, a presence, an absence?

I put this question to the congregation in a Sunday morning service at St Luke's. I gave everyone, including the children, two minutes to draw a picture of God. The only requirement was to be spontaneous and draw whatever came to mind without worrying about theology or the quality of the art. But it had to be completed in two minutes.

Some of the adults grimaced, though virtually everyone took part. The children on the other hand dived in without hesitation, starting to draw their pictures before I even finished talking.

For the most part the children drew faces and figures, many with beards. A couple of drawings featured female-looking figures. One child drew a delightful cat, another, an intriguing genie popping out of a bottle with two faces (one male, one female?). Seven-year-old Daniel began by drawing some clouds but then stopped, changing his mind. He then handed me the paper blank side up. As I made to turn it over Daniel stopped me and said, 'No, that side, Dave. It's air. God is air.'

The content of the adult drawings varied massively. As well as a few human figures of mixed gender, many people

31

drew mountains, or trees, or the sea. Some produced planets in space, or a pair of hands holding the earth. Several created shapes such as hearts, or spirals, or just had a dot indicating infinity. There were various brave attempts to convey 'God is everywhere'. The sun appeared in many of the drawings, with light radiating across the paper. One of my favourites was a picture of a dog with the words 'The only thing that could get through to me when I was suffering.'

Studies analysing children's pictures of God date back to the mid-1940s. In each survey, children below the age of six generally draw faces, while children between the ages of six and ten draw faces and people. God is often portrayed as a protector or a king, sometimes living in a palace or in the clouds. By about the age of sixteen, faces and figures mostly give way to symbols like the sun, or concentric circles, and spirals. In all the studies, the use of symbols increases with age.

Ongoing research demonstrates that everyone has some mental image of God, including atheists, even if represented by a blank page. Most of us have multiple images of God, some of which are hidden from our consciousness but can be uncovered in counselling or therapy.

To a neuroscientist, this suggests that everyone – believers and non-believers alike – may harbour a 'God neuron' or a 'God circuit' inside the brain that fires when we are asked to visualise God. For one person, such a neuron might connect with feelings of pleasure and awe, for another, with feelings of disappointment or pain. The basis of these neural connections probably traces back to images of God introduced in childhood.[*]

But due to the brain's amazing plasticity, neurons do not have to be fixed properties. They change all the time. We can reinvent God, based on different information and experiences. It apparently takes less than two weeks for a neuron to grow new axons and dendrites, and in some cases the change occurs suddenly – even a rousing sermon can trigger a rapid rewiring of circuits! For Brenda, who I mentioned at the end of the last chapter, the transformation was sparked by her reimagining God through the lens of her grandma instead of her father.

Neuroscience is not interested in theological conjecture about the nature of God, or even in whether God is real, but simply in how people *experience* God, and how this relates to the brain, and ultimately to the whole of life. For some people, the word 'God' evokes a negative

---

[*] The neurological insights in this chapter owe much to Andrew Newberg and Mark Robert Waldman, *How God Changes Your Brain* (Ballantine Books, 2010), and Andrew Newberg, *Principles of Neurotheology* (Ashgate, 2010).

neurological response, for others, a sense of happiness and peace. Either way, our images of God are never of mere intellectual or theological consequence, but significantly affect the way we think and feel about ourselves and the world.

For this reason, when I am counselling a person I often try to detect the images of God held in their conscious or unconscious mind. I tend not to ask about it directly. I am more interested in how God 'turns up' in the conversation: in passing comments and references, or in the emotional energy that surfaces when the person discusses God-stuff.

A great deal of some people's inner suffering traces back to unhealthy (but often hidden) notions of God. I regularly hear people say things like: 'Why is God putting me through this?', or 'What is God trying to teach me?', or 'Can't God see that I've suffered enough?' If asked, most of these people would say that God loves them, yet their actual experience seems to contradict this. In practice, their God appears to have a sadistic personality: on the one hand loving them, on the other, tormenting or 'testing' them.

We mostly assume that everyone means roughly the same thing by the word 'God'. A team of sociologists at Baylor University in Texas decided to explore whether this is true. They asked a nationally representative sample of American people to describe which qualities or characteristics symbolised their notion of God. Some people pictured God as kindly and loving, but twice as many thought of God as stern and punitive. Some saw God as distant and unconcerned, but many others felt that God was closely involved with their lives. The study concluded that American people tend to embrace one of four distinct personalities of God: authoritarian, critical, distant or benevolent.[*]

The Authoritarian God

Thirty-two per cent of Americans experience a God who is angry and willing to punish people who are unfaithful, or who step out of line or act in an 'ungodly' fashion. Retribution may be levelled on a large scale through social disorder or natural disasters, or on a personal scale through illness and misfortune.

This sort of authoritarian God turns up in parts of the Old Testament where God strikes down individuals, or sends plagues on nations, or sanctions the slaughter of hordes of innocent people.

---

[*] Paul Froese and Christopher Bader, *America's Four Gods: What We Say about God – & What That Says about Us* (Oxford University Press, 2010).

Yet followers of the authoritarian God are just as likely to speak of him (and he is definitely male) as loving and compassionate. Interestingly, they find no contradiction between these two very different traits of character and behaviour.

The Critical God

Another 16 per cent of Americans also believe in divine judgement but think that God rarely intervenes in earthly affairs, choosing instead to reserve vengeance for the afterlife. The Baylor research noted that ostracised ethnic minorities, the poor and the exploited often trust in this sort of God. Faced with injustice in the here and now, but seeing no payback, they take comfort in the idea that God will pass judgement in another life when all wrongs will be righted, all evil punished.

The Distant God

The second largest group, comprising 24 per cent of the American population, sees God as distant and uninvolved. God is a cosmic force that set the laws of nature in motion, but does not really 'do' things in the world. People who believe in a distant God may not even conceive of God as an entity, much less as a being with human characteristics. Almost half of those who perceive God as distant never go to church, yet almost one-third of all American Catholics, Protestants and Jews believe in a God who is distant. They rarely speak of miracles or judgement, and hardly ever pray. However, they are quite likely to practise meditation and detect a Higher Power revealed, for example, in the beauty of nature.

The Benevolent God

In contrast to the 72 per cent who believe in an authoritative, critical or distant God, just 23 per cent of Americans see God as gentle, forgiving and less likely to respond with wrath. Followers of a benevolent God have the sense that God is active in their lives and in the world, that God listens and responds to prayers, and cares about human suffering.

Both the authoritative and the benevolent gods are assumed to intervene in human affairs but in different ways. In the face of tragedy, for example, someone with an authoritative view of God is likely to believe that God either caused or allowed the tragedy in order to teach someone a lesson. Someone with a benevolent vision of God, however, is unlikely to see God's hand in the actual tragedy, but instead sees evidence of God's presence in stories of amazing coincidences or apparent miracles that saved people in the midst of disaster.

In their book *How God Changes Your Brain*, Andrew Newberg and Mark Waldman make the point that the personality we assign to God has distinct neural patterns that connect with our own emotional styles of behaviour. So, for example, in the Baylor research, most of those who embraced an authoritarian God tended to favour the death penalty, and wanted to increase the budget for the military or to give the government more power to fight terrorism. Those who perceived God as distant, on the other hand, were more open-minded than others when it came to things like gay rights, abortion and pre-marital sex.

Visualising an authoritarian or critical God will activate the limbic areas of the brain that generate fear and anger. But when we perceive God as a benevolent force, a different part of the brain is aroused in the prefrontal cortex. Loving or compassionate images and thoughts activate a circuit that involves a tiny area of the front of the brain called the anterior cingulate, which suppresses the impulse to get angry or frightened while also generating feelings of empathy towards others who are suffering or hurt.

Newberg and Waldman suggest that the anterior cingulate is the true 'heart' of our neurological soul, and when this part of the brain is stimulated, we will feel greater tolerance and acceptance towards others who hold different beliefs. The God of the limbic areas of the brain is a frightening, threatening God, but the God of the anterior cingulate is loving and empathetic.

Newberg and Waldman also identify a fifth personality of God which they think the Baylor research missed because its questions assumed that participants would think of God as a separate entity in humanlike form (father, mother, king etc.), and therefore left little scope for unitary experiences or a more mystical sense of God as a presence throughout the universe.

The Mystical God

The mystical God is less a separate entity in the universe, and more a force or presence permeating everything. People who identify with this vision of divinity (they may be more comfortable speaking about 'the divine' than 'God') use words like peace, energy and tranquillity to describe their experience of God. The mystical God is neither 'he' nor 'she', is not punitive, critical or distant.

People who embrace the mystical God are likely to be accepting of religious differences and willing to sample other spiritual traditions and beliefs. It is a conception of God that is more likely to chime with the many people who describe themselves as spiritual but not religious.

Within a specifically Christian framework, the mystical personality of God equates with Paul's statement in the New Testament that in God 'we live and move and have our being'. It also echoes the idea of divine immanence (the belief that God is present everywhere, within the very fabric of the cosmos), and with the vision of the Holy Spirit as the life-giving breath of the universe. Actually, I think seven-year-old Daniel expressed it perfectly when he said that God is air – God is all around us and within – a pretty astonishing vision of God for a seven-year-old.

Of course, research tends to put us into categories. In practice, I suspect few of us will identify entirely with any single one of these five personalities of God. We pick and mix, and also add other elements from our insights and personal experiences. No two people perceive God or the world in precisely the same way, because no two human brains begin with the same genetic code or have identical life experiences. As a neuroscientist deeply involved with brain scan technology, Andrew Newberg believes that as scan technology develops we will discover that each human being has a unique neural fingerprint that represents his or her image of God.

Yet it is also clear that just as human personalities evolve, so does one's concept of God. And Newberg suggests that the different personalities of God – authoritarian, critical, distant, benevolent and mystical – correlate to the neurological evolution and development of the brain. Indeed, he goes so far as to argue that authoritarian gods are associated with the oldest, most primitive structures of the brain, whereas a benevolent or mystical notion of God is experienced through the most recently evolved parts of the brain: structures that appear to be unique to human beings.

Newberg's developmental view of the brain appears to parallel the cultural evolution of religious traditions throughout the world. As he says, the mythological gods of nearly every tribal community had nasty personalities. Zeus was a bully hurling thunderbolts from the sky. The Aztec gods were bloodthirsty deities requiring a constant diet of human sacrifice, and the God of the Hebrews wiped out nearly every human creature with a massive flood because he judged that human ways were evil. Then, as societies and religions have developed, kinder gods have emerged. That said, the violent side to authoritarian religion still rears its head in terrorist atrocities, religious oppression of minorities, and totalitarian dogma. The old gods often linger in the subconscious waiting to re-emerge.

Even within the Bible we discover a multiplicity of images of God. And there is the distinct sense that the notion of God evolves over time. In his book *God: A Biography*, Jack Miles specifically examines how God is depicted in the Old Testament. He makes the surprising discovery that the early books of the Bible contain no real evidence of God feeling love for humanity. It is not until God declares 'everlasting love' for Israel in Isaiah 54 (two-thirds of the way through the Old Testament) that such an emotion is revealed in the text. I am not convinced that Miles's analysis is entirely correct, but it is very substantially true.

> *Until this point in history, the Lord God has never loved. Love has never been predicated of him either as an action or as a motive. It is not that he has no emotional life of any sort. He has been wrathful, vengeful, and remorseful. But he has not been loving. It was not for love that he had made man. It was not for love that he made his covenant with Abraham. It was not for love that he brought the Israelites out of Egypt or drove out the Canaanites before them.**

Yet when we come to the New Testament we encounter a God of boundless love, revealed most vividly in the figure

---

* Jack Miles, *God: A Biography* (Simon & Schuster, 1995).

of Jesus, the supreme symbol of divine love in the Christian narrative.

Certainly, on a personal level, the notion of God evolves – or should evolve – with time. Initially, our image of God tends to mirror our parents, and this forges an instinctive picture of God that, for better or worse, lodges in the psyche. For Brenda, the childhood sense that God was like her critical, vindictive father blighted her life for years. Whereas in my own experience, the feeling which I grew up with, that God was like my mother who loved me unconditionally, produced a persistent source of empowerment and reassurance.

Time and again I try to help people to reinvent some of their entrenched notions of God: to dump critical, punitive and undermining images (often based on parents, teachers, vicars and other authority figures) and replace them with the sense of a loving, compassionate and empowering presence in their life.

In some instances, I explicitly encourage people to reimagine God in their own ethnic likeness: to picture God, for example, as a black woman or man. I feel devastated that so many non-white people I have talked with over the years pictured God as a white male. I recently encouraged a young Asian woman to adopt a spiritual practice of drawing pictures of God as an Asian mother-figure, as a way of loving herself, loving her ethnicity, loving her genetic heritage – and discovering in the process an entirely different experience of God. How can any of us sense that we are beloved children of God if we experience God as ethnically and culturally alien?

Of course, God is no more (or less!) an Asian woman than a European man. God surpasses categories of race and gender. Yet the heart of the Christian message is that God penetrates and inhabits humanity: not one particular strand of humanity, one gender or ethnicity, but all of humanity. The Christian affirmation that God indwelt Jesus Christ does not mean that God is a first-century Jewish man, but that God becomes flesh and blood time and again in every expression of humanity: male and female, gay and straight, black and white, rich and poor, Christian, Muslim, Hindu and atheist.

We have a natural propensity to turn God into an image, to create symbols, mental pictures and verbal constructions of our notion of God. This is perfectly normal and fine. The problem arises when we believe that our images and conceptions of God are literally true, that we can actually describe who or what God is. At that point religion turns into idolatry; we replace that which is infinite and indescribable with something finite and ephemeral. C.S. Lewis identifies this temptation and wrestles with it sublimely in his little piece 'Footnote to all Prayers':

> He whom I bow to only knows to whom I bow
> When I attempt the ineffable Name, murmuring Thou,
> And dream of Pheidian fancies and embrace in heart
> Symbols (I know) which cannot be the thing Thou art.
> Thus always, taken at their word, all prayers blaspheme
> Worshipping with frail images a folk-lore dream,
> And all men in their praying, self-deceived, address
> The coinage of their own unquiet thoughts, unless
> Thou in magnetic mercy to Thyself divert
> Our arrows, aimed unskillfully, beyond desert;
> And all men are idolaters, crying unheard
> To a deaf idol, if Thou take them at their word.
> Take not, O Lord, our literal sense. Lord, in thy great
> Unbroken speech our limping metaphor translate.*

Lewis admits that all God-talk, all language and imagery to describe God is hopelessly inadequate: 'frail images' and 'limping metaphors' which cannot be the thing that God is. Every scrap of religious language – visual and

---

* C. S. Lewis, *Selected Books: The Pilgrim's Regress / Prayer: Letter to Malcolm / Reflections on the Psalms / Till We Have Faces / The Abolition of Man* (HarperCollins, 2011).

45

verbal – is but a human device to address that which is utterly beyond our comprehension. And yet Lewis does not rubbish God-talk, simply sees it for what it is.

So how do we hold these two things together: our need for God to have a face that we can comprehend and relate to, and the reality that God transcends every visual and verbal representation that we can possibly conceive?

I like Marcus Borg's idea of differentiating between a 'wholesale' and a 'retail' vision of God.* The 'wholesale God' is the God we cannot describe, God beyond all names and designations – God beyond 'God'. This God does not exist, but is existence itself, the ultimate reality within and beyond all that is.

The 'retail' God is God with a face and a name, the God of biblical stories and church liturgy, the God we know as father, mother, lover, shepherd, deliverer. The God named differently in different religious traditions. Typically, though not always, the 'retail God' is personified, and these personifications become the natural language of prayer, devotion and church language. 'Retail' religion involves speaking to, or about, God with the sense that God is a being with some likeness to ourselves.

But is God personal? I certainly *experience* God as

---

* Marcus Borg, *The Heart of Christianity* (HarperOne, 2011).

personal. However, I don't think that the only alternative to 'personal' is 'impersonal'. I prefer to think of God as *trans*personal or *supra*-personal. By this I mean that God is *everything we can imagine and include within the notion of personhood – and much more.*

When we experience the 'retail God' we experience empathy, compassion, healing and hope, we shout and sing and celebrate God's love. When we experience God as the 'wholesale God' we experience mystery, a 'deep and dazzling darkness', the 'cloud of unknowing'; we sense reverence, awe and wonder; our God-talk diminishes, we are reduced to silence.

I have no problem with the 'retail' version of God; I am the vicar of a parish church, a 'retail outlet'. I am comfortable with personal references to God, with metaphors that describe God as 'shepherd', 'deliverer', 'mother', 'father' etc. I use 'retail God' language all the time. It is not literally true. Of course it isn't. God is not a man or a woman, a king or a queen. Yet this does not mean that retail language is *un*true. When we say that we love someone with all our heart, it may be profoundly true, but it's not literally true. Only crude fundamentalism (religious and non-religious) requires literal fact as the basis for truth.

But when all is said and done, I find that I encounter

God most powerfully in people. And the babe of Bethlehem remains the most vivid symbol of how the divine appears in the most unexpected forms, in the most surprising circumstances, as when I went to see Jim about his wife Ethel's funeral.

It was the end of a long and busy day. I was tired, and looking forward to getting my shoes off with a glass of red wine and a bit of TV with Pat. I tramped my way through the large block of flats searching for number whatever it was. 'It won't take long,' I thought. 'Let's get it over with.'

When Jim opened the door, I realised it would take a bit longer than I had hoped. Jim wasn't in a mood for hurrying. So I agreed to a cup of tea (the fifteenth of the day!), which took ten minutes to brew. I sat still, waiting, but agitated and impatient on the inside. When Jim returned, he said he'd forgotten that I was coming. 'I've just got back from the home where she's been staying with bags of her stuff,' he said. 'Not very pleasant.'

In that moment of understated devastation – 'Not very pleasant' – I woke up on the inside. My blind eyes were opened. I saw a lovely, grieving man who'd lost his bride of sixty years! And I felt Jesus, crucified afresh in Jim's grief. I love my job, but somehow – tiredness, impatience, eagerness to veg out in front of the TV – I'd elbowed Jim into the margins. But now I felt I was in a holy place. I wanted to remove my shoes for a different reason. I felt honoured to be there. I stayed for quite a long time. We looked through his CDs to find some songs for the funeral. His eye twinkled as he told me about their night at the Royal Festival Hall to see Frank Sinatra. 'He walked on stage right past us,' Jim said. 'We could have touched him.'

I left Jim's house that night glowing with humble gratitude. I'd thought I was doing a routine funeral visit at the end of the day. But in fact I encountered the suffering Christ who was present in Jim's bereavement. To paraphrase the words of Jesus in one of his parables: 'I was bereft and you gave me comfort.'* I met God in an old man, heartbroken for the wife of his youth.

Who could call this work?

* Matthew 25:34–45.

4. God on the brain

religion and spiritual intelligence

*Your vision of God depends on where you are in
your spiritual development.*

Ken Wilber

I first met Angie after one of my seminars. She stood in
front of me and baldly announced, 'My son is a Buddhist
and my daughter is in an ashram!'

'Wow! Aren't you lucky?' I enthused (not knowing
whether she saw it as a good thing or a bad).

'AM I?' she replied, smiling inquisitively.

'Absolutely,' I said. 'You have two amazing kids on wonderful spiritual journeys. How fantastic is that? You must be delighted.'

We laughed and became great friends. And if Angie did have concerns about her children's spiritual proclivities, she certainly does not have them now. Angie and her lovely husband Ken are the proudest parents on God's earth, awestruck at what Guy and Nessie have become. And little wonder!

In 2010 Guy joined a couple of friends to launch Planetary Collective, an exciting group of young filmmakers, visual media specialists, and creative thinkers who work with cosmologists, ecologists and philosophers in exploring some of the big questions facing our planet. In 2012, they released a short documentary film called *Overview* about the experiences of astronauts in space and how seeing the earth from the outside transformed their vision of the planet and humankind's place upon it. The award-winning film is in fact a prelude to an even more ambitious project: a feature-length documentary entitled *Planetary* intended to help kick-start a new way of thinking about our relationship with our fellow human beings and the planet.[*]

---

[*] *Overview Effect* and a trailer of *Planetary* can be accessed at www.planetarycollective.com, and http://planetary.vhx.tv

As I write, Nessie has just returned from a course at Bern University where she joined nineteen other young environmentalists from around the world, trying to find solutions to poverty. She is already a passionate human rights activist, a defender of rainforests, an inspiring yoga teacher, and an all-round beautiful human being. And she is just getting started!

Guy and Nessie are smart, imaginative and extremely energetic. More than that, they have spiritual nous: a sense of what matters in life: an awareness of the 'big picture' – for themselves and the world and their place and purpose in it. This has nothing to do with whether they are Buddhist, Hindu, Christian, Muslim, Jew or atheist. It's more basic than that. It's about spiritual intelligence – a quality that transcends religious beliefs and affiliations yet which lies at the heart of every religious tradition.

For much of the twentieth century intelligence was measured purely on the basis of a person's intellectual skills, signified by an IQ score. However, following Howard Gardner's ground-breaking book *Frames of Mind: The Theory of Multiple Intelligence*, published in the mid-1980s, we now recognise a host of different kinds of intelligence, including physical, mental, emotional and spiritual. And many see spiritual intelligence as central and most fundamental because it becomes a source of guidance to all the intelligences.

Spiritual intelligence (SQ) has no necessary connection to religion, although it may be channelled through a particular religious tradition. It neither requires nor precludes belief in God. And in a sense, it precedes religious belief because it represents the part of us that seeks religious meaning in the first place. Many humanists and atheists have very high SQ; many actively religious people have very low SQ.

SQ is the intelligence that enables us to place our lives in a wider, richer, meaningful context. It's the intelligence we use when we ask 'why' rather than merely 'what' or 'how'. It represents our drive for meaning and value, and connection with the infinite. When we ponder a moral dilemma, or try to make sense of a harrowing situation, we exercise spiritual intelligence. When we sense wonder and awe, or feel a deep connectedness with people or the world, we exercise spiritual intelligence.*

So far as we know, we are the only creatures with this capacity. When I climb a hill or walk in the woods I sometimes wonder about the meaning of life, but my beautiful dog Woody never gives it a moment's thought. He just

---

* Danah Zohar and Ian Marshall, *SQ: Connecting with our Spiritual Intelligence* (Bloomsbury, 2000).

sniffs through the undergrowth, pees everywhere and chases squirrels. Human beings are meaning-seeking animals; though it is up to each of us to decide how much meaning we seek, how much SQ we choose to draw on.

Features of high-level SQ activity include:

- *Self-awareness – a grasp of what makes us tick, in terms of values and motivations.*
- *Constancy – consistency in following our deepest convictions and values – even when it means standing against the crowd.*
- *Spontaneity – staying alive in the moment and responding to what each moment presents.*
- *Empathy – identifying with others and sharing in their feelings.*
- *Humility – a measured sense of our own place in the wider scheme of things.*
- *Curiosity – the motivation to explore – especially the 'why?' questions.*
- *Flexibility – standing back from a situation or problem to see the bigger picture, and make necessary readjustments.*
- *Resilience – remaining positive in the face of adversity; learning and growing from mistakes and setbacks.*

- *Groundedness – a sense of bearing and purpose.*
- *Receptivity – staying open and welcoming towards diversity and difference.*

Arguably, the most important question in the entire process of engaging our spiritual intelligence is this: what sort of person do I wish to be? It is a question most of us seldom call to mind, yet which we answer many times every day in the decisions and choices we make. It literally shapes our life, so it is worth pausing occasionally to give it some conscious thought.

One of the simplest ways to do this is to spend a few minutes listing the people you admire most in the world, and then identify what it is about them that you admire. The obvious starting place for most of us is people like Nelson Mandela, Martin Luther King, Jesus and the Dalai Lama. But if we stick with the question, we will start thinking about other people closer to home: a grandparent, a friend, an old teacher, a work colleague, our partner etc.

Among the hundreds of people I have asked to do this, the descriptions of what they admire in their heroes is reassuringly similar:

- their compassion and kindness
- their courage in the face of conflict

- their ability to forgive and move on
- their modesty and humility
- their sense of peace in the midst of turmoil
- their honesty and integrity
- their cheerfulness in times of adversity
- their creativity and imagination.

One of my own long-standing role models is the late Anwar Sadat, president of Egypt, who collaborated with former Israeli Prime Minister Menachem Begin and US President Jimmy Carter to create the Camp David Peace Accords in the late 1970s. I recall weeping when I saw pictures of Sadat and Begin on the television holding hands and smiling at one another, with Jimmy Carter grinning in the background, looking spookily like the minister at a wedding.

Paving the way for the accord, Sadat travelled to Israel to address the Knesset, the Israeli parliament. It was a bold and courageous move. In his speech there he lamented the loss of every life in the Middle East conflict, Arab and Israeli. He said that it was essential for people of wisdom and vision on both sides to move beyond the past and reach towards new horizons.

In earlier times Sadat had toured Egypt as a popular Arab leader, declaring that he would NEVER! NEVER!

NEVER! shake the hand of an Israeli. The crowds chanted back, 'NEVER! NEVER! NEVER!' Yet Sadat made a total U-turn, shaking the hands of countless Israelis.

In his memoir, he talks about his imprisonment and solitary confinement as a young man in Cairo. He writes: 'My contemplation of life and human nature in that secluded place, taught me that he who cannot change the very fabric of his thought will never be able to change reality, and will never, therefore, make any progress.'

Bestselling business author Stephen Covey recounts having lunch with Sadat's wife, Madame Jehan Sadat, and asking her what it was like living with her husband at the time when he decided to visit Israel. She confessed to having a hard time believing his change of heart, and related her conversation with him, which went something like:

'I understand you are thinking of going to Israel. Is this correct?'

'Yes.'

'How could you possibly do this after all you have been saying?'

'I was wrong, and this is the right thing to do.'

'You will lose the leadership and support of the Arab world.'

'I suppose that could happen; but I don't think it will.'

'You will lose the presidency of your country.'

'That too could happen.'

'You'll lose your life.'

'My life is ordained. It will not be one minute longer or one minute shorter than it was ordained to be.'

At that point, his wife embraced him and said he was the greatest person she had ever known.*

A squad of Egyptian soldiers assassinated Anwar Sadat on 6 October 1981. But now, decades later, I am still hugely inspired by his capacity to transcend his own ego, to set aside political and religious dogma, even to disregard his own safety for what he believed. He was a man of great stature, spiritually as well as politically. I may not share his religion but I absolutely aspire to his wisdom and spiritual intelligence.

Many people confuse being spiritual with being religious, but they are quite different things. Religion is a systematic set of beliefs, practices and rituals, which we may grow up with, or adopt as adults. Spiritual

---

* Stephen Covey, *The 8th Habit: From Effectiveness to Greatness* (Simon & Schuster, 2004).

intelligence, on the other hand, is an intrinsic capacity hardwired into the human brain, which we choose to nurture and cultivate, or to neglect.

I tend not to admire a person for their theological beliefs, but for the wisdom and spiritual intelligence with which they practise their beliefs. And frankly, I sometimes find a greater kindred spirit with someone of a different faith than with someone of my own – as did Jesus when he praised a pagan Roman centurion for having more faith (spiritual nous) than his fellow Jews.

I find it particularly frustrating to see spiritually intelligent non-churchgoers rub up against spiritually dumb attitudes and policies within the church, which is precisely what happened when John and Sophie approached their local vicar about having their two-year-old daughter Gabriella christened.

Despite not being regulars at the church, John and Sophie hoped for a warm reception. And things appeared to go well until they revealed their carefully drawn-up list of godparents, which included a Jewish man and a Hindu woman. Both of these deeply spiritual people clearly understood the meaning and responsibility of being a godparent, and were very happy to encourage Gabriella in the Christian faith. However, given the general expectation in the church that godparents will be baptised

Christians, it was a situation that required some spiritual nous and a little liturgical flexibility. Sadly both were lacking. The baptism could not go ahead. Though, ironically, it probably would have been permitted had the godparents been nominal Christians who happened to be baptised.

Thinking the door to the church was closed to them, John and Sophie decided to organise a naming ceremony instead. But a mutual friend suggested that they talk with me first, to see if I would conduct the christening. After meeting them I enthusiastically agreed, fully persuaded that all four candidates would make excellent godparents.

The christening was a joyful occasion: sixty people gathered around the font celebrating a beautiful young life, joyfully welcomed into the family of the church. Afterwards, over a meal in a local tapas restaurant, I enjoyed numerous warm conversations with people who found the whole event spiritually uplifting. 'I'm not really religious,' one man said, 'but that was the best religious experience I have ever had.'

A couple of weeks later, I received a card from Gabriella (penned by her mum, naturally), which read:

Thank you for my very special Christening with the lovely songs and candles. I may not remember it, but

Mama says my spirit will, and it marked my soul in some way. I don't know what she means, but it made her and Dada happy, so I'm happy too. I am a very blessed girl because my life is full of love and special people like you . . .

Sophie added, 'I hope this card will remind you of the young soul you served with that wonderful service at St Luke's.'

> *SQ takes us to the heart of things, to the unity behind difference, to the potential beyond any actual expression. SQ can put us in touch with the meaning and essential spirit behind all great religions. A person high in SQ might practice any religion, but without narrowness, exclusiveness, bigotry or prejudice.*
>
> *Danah Zohar**

The way that religion is practised reflects a particular notion or vision of God. If the only God on offer were a nit-picking rules enforcer, I for one would instantly become an atheist. But this is not the case. There are many visions of God. And, in fact, the kind of God we

---

* Danah Zohar and Ian Marshall, *Connecting with our Spiritual Intelligence* (Bloomsbury: New York, 2000).

believe in probably says more about our own spiritual development than it says about the actual nature of the divine. SQ does not determine *whether* we will believe in God, but it massively affects the *sort* of God we can believe in.

The psychotherapist and writer M. Scott Peck, who basically saw therapy as an exercise in personal and spiritual development, made the fascinating observation that when people who were deeply religious entered therapy with him, they frequently left the process as agnostics or atheists. But agnostics and atheists often ended up becoming deeply religious. This puzzled him to begin with – same process, same therapist but entirely different religious outcomes – until he realised that people are not all in the same place spiritually.

For some people, spiritual progress requires leaving behind a notion of God that now appears naïve or downright unsustainable. But for others, it may mean opening up to the possibility of faith: to a vision of divinity not previously contemplated. 'When I was a child,' St Paul says, 'I spoke like a child, I thought like a child, I reasoned like a child; when I became an adult, I put an end to childish ways.'* Both belief and unbelief in God may be noth-

---

* 1 Corinthians 13:11.

ing more than a hand-me-down 'childish' way of thinking which we need to outgrow.

Developing SQ requires authenticity, which is what real faith is about. Faith does not require us to believe six impossible things before breakfast; it requires us to be authentic human beings committed to what we believe to be of ultimate concern.

This is how I go about teaching people faith. I don't attempt to convince them to sign up to this or that set of beliefs, but to live honestly and authentically. I love Cindy Wigglesworth's definition of spiritual intelligence: 'The ability to behave with wisdom and compassion, while maintaining inner and outer peace, regardless of the situation.'

I hung on to this aspiration as, feeling overwhelmed by their loss, I walked into the flat where Jason and Linda live. They had tried and tried for their first baby, then it died after just three days in an incubator. We didn't even sit down, just stood there in the kitchen, fighting back the tears, all three of us. Linda said, 'I'm not very religious, Dave. Please don't ask me to believe in God or anything. But I do want you to take the funeral.'

'As it happens, I'm one of the least religious priests you could find,' I told her. 'And I'm certainly not going to ask you to believe anything.'

64

A few days after the funeral, we were in the kitchen again – sitting down this time. The tears were dried up, replaced with steely rage. 'My aunt who is religious told me that God moves in mysterious ways,' Linda said. 'And I told her, "F**k your stupid God!"'

We sat in silence for a while. Linda apologised and asked, 'Do you think I'm awful, Dave?'

'I think you're very hurt,' I said, 'and probably a bit too restrained. I hope that's not because the vicar's here . . . because if I were you, I'd probably be shouting and cursing and kicking everything in the room. And if I believed in a God who hangs about making "mysterious" decisions about whether little babies live or die I'd probably be out burning churches and kicking priests . . . but I don't believe in that sort of God.'

Linda and Jason still don't believe in God, as such. But I am not trying to change that. My only interest is in helping them to process their feelings honestly, in the hope that they will gradually open themselves to the prospect of living again, and maybe find the courage to try for another baby. Because when we find the courage to live, to embrace new possibilities while at the same time risking further disappointment, we grow spiritually. We also start to understand the meaning of faith – to entrust ourselves to life's immensity.

5. God is what grabs you deep down
faith without creeds

If one thinks that Christianity consists solely in doctrinal precision, the Christian mystery becomes a pious fable.

Gregory of Nyssa

Victoria Willson died in September 2013, aged forty-three. I was privileged to conduct her funeral at St Luke's Church. Victoria was born with a condition called tuberous sclerosis, which causes growths on the brain, and led to a profound learning disability. She wasn't supposed to live this long. But no one told her that. She just got on with life, achieving more than most people do in twice the time.

At the funeral, her mother, Jean, described Victoria as a 'woman without words', communicating mainly by flexing her eyebrows. But she knew what she wanted, 'and if we did not understand then she pinched and pulled our hair until we got it right'. She also threw things and shouted.

Everyone who knew Victoria loved her. She was a gorgeous, flirtatious, flamboyant woman with hundreds of friends and many more admirers. Her passion was music, from Madonna to Mozart. She dressed in bold and brightly coloured clothes, wore nail varnish, and enjoyed food, good company and going for walks. She also loved swimming, splashing about, and drinking by the pool.

When she was younger, the medical authorities wanted to institutionalise Victoria, but her mother had none of it. 'I wouldn't leave my cat here,' Jean told a consultant when looking around the long-stay mental handicap hospital. Together Jean and Victoria battled with the local authorities and finally succeeded in persuading them to move Victoria into a converted bungalow to live with a friend and two carers. As the true pioneer and innovator, Victoria showed the world that she could live safely, happily and independently in her own home.

Together, mother and daughter launched countless campaigns such as 'Save a Baby', 'Treat me Right', 'Death by Indifference', 'Stand by Me' and 'Changing Places' that have contributed to improving the lives of many people with multiple and complex needs.

In North London, Jean is a local hero, not just because of her courage and tenacity in caring for a daughter with an intense disability, but because she became a champion for multitudes of other people with disabilities and their families.

In 2010, Jean was presented with a coveted Woman of the Year award, and later received an OBE from the Queen, and the Freedom of the Borough of Islington. None of this in any way deflects her from her single-minded mission. For more than forty years Jean has worked with Centre 404, a grass-roots charity based in a large house across the road from where I live which coordinates help for thousands of the borough's disabled and their parents and carers.

Jean doesn't see herself as a hero. Of course she doesn't. She is just a mother who decided that her child, and other children like her, deserved better. And she would say that her achievements owe much to her lovely husband Norman as well as their older daughter, Tara.

A few days after the funeral, Jean and Tara came to a service at St Luke's. She told me afterwards, 'I'm not a woman of faith, Dave, but I am a woman of action.' My sermon that morning happened to be based on the words of St James: 'Show me your faith without works, and I by my works will show you my faith.'[*] Afterwards I got to thinking that if Jean Willson is not a woman of faith in the truest and best sense, then I don't know what faith is. Every time I step into Centre 404 I feel as if I am entering the *real* church, with Jean as its 'priest'.

On occasions when I hear the sound of partying coming from the centre – which seems to be quite often – I look out of my study window to glimpse a glorious mixture of people often made to feel like misfits and outsiders in society, celebrating and having fun. And I smile and think to myself: *that* is the kingdom of God, right there; that is what Jesus talked about and made a reality: a fellowship of mutual empowerment, a symbol of hope and freedom; what Martin Luther King called 'the beloved community'.

Jean is a woman of obvious spiritual intelligence: someone driven to transform the world in accordance

---

* James 2:18.

with her instinctive sense of how things should be. She has a vision of compassion and justice triumphing over prejudice and discrimination, and pursues it tenaciously.

But is she a woman of faith? That depends on what you mean by faith. Paul Tillich said that faith is the state of being 'ultimately concerned'; of being gripped and driven by something that we are convinced is of fundamental importance, and which demands our wholehearted commitment. If Tillich is right, then Jean has faith by the barrowful – as do many people who will never appear in church or make any particular claim to being religious.

Everyone experiences concerns: for themselves, for loved ones, for the world in general. But beyond these, human beings have a unique and compelling concern to make sense of life, to establish meaning and value, to understand why we exist in the first place and to try to mould our world accordingly. When we become caught up with this, when we are gripped by our ultimate concern, Tillich argues that we experience faith – not in the specific sense of being a Christian, a Muslim or a Hindu, say, but in a universal or generic sense.

Once we exercise spiritual intelligence, once we begin to pursue meaning in life – once we become caught up with things of ultimate (and not merely mundane) concern, we start to encounter what I name as 'God'. Constantly, in the course of my work, I speak with people who tell me that while they don't go to church or see themselves as religious, they know that there is 'something there', something more to life to be sought and grappled with, something to be reached out to. 'God or whatever,' I hear people say. And it is in times of crisis, pain or great joy, in the threshold experiences of life like birth and death, that we tend to sense most vividly this 'something there'.

Yet the fact remains, that for increasing numbers of people the term 'God' just no longer works as a way of describing this 'something'. So I often say to people, forget 'God', forget religious jargon and translate the 'something' into terms that make sense to you. But whatever you do, do not lose sight of the ultimate concern. Keep journeying with what you sense to be truly fundamental in life. Allow that to shape who you are and what you do.

Yet, as I have already expressed in this book, my frustration is that, often, people's struggle with the 'G' word is based on a misunderstanding that the only way to think about God is within a literalistic theistic framework. In other words, to see God as a supernatural humanlike being 'out there', someone who 'made' the universe

– perhaps in six days – and intervenes, or gets involved with its workings, from time to time.

Our friend, Jenny, is a good example of someone who just could not get past this sort of vision of God. Before she died, she used to stay in our home a couple of times each year when she visited London with her work. Invariably, we would end up having deep conversations well into the night, often consuming more red wine than we should. Jenny didn't have a religious bone in her body, but she had a great zest for life, and a passion for justice in the world. She was a woman of deep spirituality, if not religion, and we shared a lot in common.

However, in one conversation, at about 2.30am, she seemed agitated and concerned that our views might be converging a little too much. Sipping nervously on her wine she said, 'But you need to remember, Dave: I am an atheist.'

'You're about as much an atheist as I am an atheist,' I pronounced with the kind of pomposity I only ever attain under the influence of alcohol.

'How do you make that out?' she replied.

'Because you are one of the most spiritually motivated people I know,' I said. 'And, ultimately, we believe in the same thing. It's just that I call it God and you don't.'

73

That was the night I managed to convince Jenny that when I say 'God' I am not talking about a 'big guy upstairs'.

Jenny was a woman who wrestled with ultimate questions. She was on a faith journey – regardless of how she chose to name it. So was she really an atheist? Not in Tillich's terms. He argues that a real atheist is someone who denies that there is any ultimate concern; in other words, that life is entirely meaningless. This certainly was not Jenny. It is not most 'atheists' I know. We may not share 'God' talk, but we do share 'ultimate concern'.

When all the paraphernalia of specific religious tradition is stripped away, there are just two basic 'truths' that a genuine religious sense requires. Every other doctrine derives in some way from these.

1. Our lives are embraced by mystery

In a lovely old book entitled *Living Philosophies: A Series of Intimate Credos*, Albert Einstein wrote:

> The most beautiful thing we can experience is the mysterious. It is the source of all true art and science. He to whom the emotion is a stranger, who can no longer pause to wonder and stand wrapped in awe, is as good as dead – his eyes are closed. The insight into

the mystery of life, coupled though it be with fear, has also given rise to religion. To know what is impenetrable to us really exists, manifesting itself as the highest wisdom and the most radiant beauty, which our dull faculties can comprehend only in their most primitive forms – this knowledge, this feeling is at the center of true religiousness.

Einstein emphasised that he could not imagine a God who rewards and punishes the objects of his creation, whose purposes are modelled after our own – a God, in short, who is but a reflection of human frailty. Yet what he describes and names as 'the mysterious' equates fundamentally with my understanding of the divine.

All religions stress in some way that God is a mystery which cannot ultimately be put into words or reduced to human categories. Within Christianity the most profound understanding of God (known as the *apophatic* tradition or the *via negativa*) maintains that the closer we get to God the less we can comprehend or speak of God. To commune with the divine is in fact to enter a deep and deafening silence.

Yet each of us is embraced by this mystery, whether or not we are religious. And we become aware of it through occasional mindful epiphanies that break through our normal inattentiveness, breathing hope and warmth into the soul:

- the sense of awesome tininess when we gaze into a starry sky on a dark night;
- watching a new-born lamb struggling to find its feet for the first time;
- smelling the top of a baby's head;
- listening to the full-hearted evensong of a blackbird on a late autumn afternoon just before the sun drops;
- getting lost in a favourite piece of music;
- merging with a loved one on a settee without a word being uttered.

This knowledge, this feeling, Einstein says, is the 'center of true religiousness': to know that what is impenetrable to us really exists. One person may declare, 'The whole earth is full of God's glory',[*] another may simply draw a deep breath and feel, 'Wow! It's good to be alive!' But it is the sense of being embraced by mystery that unites us and directs us towards what Paul Tillich calls ultimate concern.

---

[*] Isaiah 6:3.

2. The mystery is gracious

Einstein also once said that the most important question facing humanity is, 'Is the universe a friendly place?' If we decide that the universe is an unfriendly place, then we will use all our resources to create bigger walls to keep out the unfriendliness, he said. And if we decide that the universe is neither friendly nor unfriendly and that God is 'playing dice with the universe', then we are simply victims to the random toss of the dice and our lives have no real purpose or meaning. But if we decide that the universe is indeed a friendly place, then we will devote ourselves to creating tools and models for understanding that universe.

As we have already noted, Einstein rejected the notion of a theistic 'big guy upstairs', but he did conclude that the universe is friendly. 'God does not play dice with the universe', he affirmed; our lives do indeed have meaning and purpose.

But is it true? Is the universe friendly? What about the 'unfriendliness' we experience in the world – not just the hostility too often found in human relations, but the brutality of sickness and suffering, and the oft-times inhospitableness of nature itself – the storms and floods, the droughts and famines etc.?

Perhaps it is more accurate to say that the universe is an ambiguously friendly place. We cannot deny that there is unfriendliness on all kinds of levels. But the greater truth is the triumph of the human spirit: people do find ways through even the most painful experiences; love does overcome evil; hope does rise in the most desperate of situations. Something embedded in the depths of human existence tells us that the mystery at the heart of the universe is trustworthy, and that our fulfilment lies in surrendering to it.

In Christianity, grace is the central expression of the divine mystery, symbolised in the self-emptying love of Christ. The crucifixion is not about an angry despotic God demanding bloodthirsty restitution through the death of his son; it's about a crucified God who is always immersed in the pain and suffering and brutality of the world. God is never distant, always present.

But we don't need to be religious to know that the mystery of life can sustain us, that we can deal with whatever comes along if we remain open and receptive to the grace rooted in the depths of existence.

From these two truths: the sense of mystery and its graciousness, we can derive all the other important ideas of religion. Religion is often made far too complicated and forbidding. The rest is important, of course it is, but all we truly need to know as human beings is that we are accepted by that which is greater than us – whose name none of us finally knows; not really.

Faith is the state of being 'ultimately concerned'; of being gripped and driven by something that we are convinced is of fundamental importance, and which places an unconditional demand upon us. Faith is also the attitude of full-hearted openness to the mystery of life – entrusting the soul to life's immensity. And sometimes that takes courage as well as vision.

I do think that Jean Willson and her husband Norman are people of faith in the truest sense, though neither of them is particularly religious. They are people who have indeed opened themselves to life's immensity.

When Victoria was born, her parents and four-year-old sister lived in a damp, rat-infested basement flat. On New Year's Eve, before she arrived, Norman remembers saying, 'Things can only get better!' That wasn't quite how it turned out. To begin with, getting rehoused proved to be an almighty struggle. Then Victoria turned out to have a profound learning difficulty. And life became very hard.

The Willsons have experienced years of battling with incompetent and unsympathetic authorities; they have dealt with ignorance, prejudice and discrimination; they have fought their way through endless setbacks and disappointment; they understand exhaustion. It would have been easy to allow circumstances to crush them, to descend into an abyss of despair and self-pity.

But they embraced life's immensity, and transformed what, at times, probably felt like an overwhelming injustice – having a child with complex and profound disabilities – into a triumph of grace and determination. Instead of feeling sorry for themselves, they came to realise that they were deeply privileged to be part of Victoria's life – 'my Wonder Woman' as Jean described her. And they managed to enrich and transform the lives of thousands of people in the process.

That is what I call faith.

And I long for more of it.

6. Did they fall, or were they pushed?

why Eve was a hero, not a villain

Most people do not really want freedom, because freedom involves responsibility, and most people are frightened of responsibility.

Sigmund Freud

It has been said that there are two religions in America, one spiritual, one secular. The first worships in churches, the other at business conventions. Clergy of both religions wear dark suits and ties (or clerical collars). They

81

both believe they have the truth that others need, and they both exchange a lot of business cards. The film *The Big Kahuna* is a fascinating observation of an uneasy confrontation between the two systems of faith.

The film is set in the hospitality suite of a tired Wichita hotel in the Midwest, where three industrial-lubricant salesmen hope to land the big sale that will shore up the ailing fortunes of their company. (Can I hear you yawning?) But, actually, the storyline is incidental to a film that turns out to be riveting. With the intimacy and intensity of a stage play, it takes place almost entirely in one room over a twenty-four-hour period, and focuses exclusively on the interaction between the three main characters.

Larry (Kevin Spacey) is edgy, sardonic, competitive and foul-mouthed, never short of a greasy one-liner. Phil (Danny DeVito), a life-weary divorcee in his mid-fifties, is still smarting from the painful breakup of his marriage – and is trying to quit drinking. Larry and Phil have been comrades in arms for a long time. Bob (Peter Facinelli), on the other hand, is a young man, fresh out of college, at his first business convention. He is a squeaky clean born-again Christian, and newly married. His religious idealism rapidly rankles with his older colleagues as he quotes the Bible, preaches his naïve brand of faith and passes judgement on what he considers their immoral ways.

Yet as events unfold, much to their surprise and irritation, Phil and Larry find themselves reliant on the young rookie when the big fish, the 'big kahuna', invites Bob (and only Bob) to an exclusive party. Awaiting his return with news that could end their careers, Phil and Larry engage in poignant conversation about God, love and the meaning of life.

Eventually, when Bob reappears hours later, he drops a bombshell: rather than trying to sell lubricants, he instead chose to talk to their target for hours about Jesus. No contracts were signed, no deal struck, no further meeting arranged. Bob didn't even get around to handing over a business card – though he apparently had a wonderful time talking about the Lord! Larry goes ballistic, then, after a heated row and some pathetic fisticuffs with Bob, disappears to bed, still fuming.

With Larry gone, Phil announces that he has something to say. With searing honesty and breath-taking wisdom, he slices through Bob's cocksure religious zeal to reveal a hollowness that Bob won't even begin to acknowledge.

'You preaching Jesus,' Phil says, 'is no different from Larry, or anybody else, preaching lubricants. It doesn't matter whether you're selling Jesus or Buddha or civil rights, or how to make money in real estate with no money down. That doesn't make you a human being; it makes you a marketing rep. If you want to talk to some-body honestly, as a human being, ask him about his kids, find out what his dreams are – just to find out, for no other reason. Because as soon as you lay your hands on a conversation to steer it, it's not a conversation any more: it's a pitch. And you're not a human being. You're a marketing rep.'

Shaken up and wiping away a tear, Bob stutters, 'Forgive me if I respectfully disagree.' Undeterred, Phil turns the conversation to character, picking up on an earlier exchange where they talked about how character can sometimes shape a person's face. 'But the question is much deeper than that,' Phil says. 'The question is: Do you have any character at all? And if you want my honest opinion, Bob, you do not – for the simple reason that you don't regret anything yet.'

'Are you saying I won't have any character unless I do something I regret?' Bob protests.

'No, Bob,' Phil says with near-fatherly compassion, 'I'm saying you've already done plenty of things to regret. You just don't know what they are.'

Washed-out, and looking like he has been squeezed through a mangle, Bob asks, 'May I leave now?'

'Go ahead,' Phil says, taking a final pull on his cigarette.

Bob departs without a word.

As he closes the door behind him, Phil wistfully mutters 'Goodnight', and picks up the whisky bottle.

This scene never fails to move me. It vividly portrays the contrast between a heavenly minded, uptight piety that I have encountered far too often, and a down-to-earth integrity issuing from hard-earned self-awareness, and broken, unpretentious humanity.[*]

Yet it is not just a contrast between two attitudes, but also between two visions of God. I find myself drawn, in real life as well as in this film, to the God I sense in the rough-and-ready humanity of an honest 'sinner', rather than to the God represented in pious religion.

Jesus told a story about two men who went up to the temple to pray, one a Pharisee and the other a tax collector.[†] The Pharisee thanked God that he was not like other people: thieves, villains, adulterers and the despised tax collector. 'I fast twice a week and give a tenth of all my income,' he declared. Meanwhile, the tax collector, showing no awareness of the Pharisee, refused even to lift his eyes to heaven, but beat his breast crying, 'God, be merciful to me a sinner!'

---

[*] You can watch this scene at http://www.youtube.com/watch?v=-PkOc-B64dY.
[†] Luke 18:13.

I'd say that Phil in the film and the tax collector in the parable are more evolved human beings, more spiritually intelligent people, than either Bob or the Pharisee – not *despite* their imperfections, but *because* of them. They know they are 'sinners'; they know they have flaws, and this allows them to transcend the ego, reaching to something greater.

I use the word 'sinner', here, grudgingly. It's a term with a cruel history, employed often to harass and burden people in Christ's name. Yet Jesus himself obviously enjoyed hanging out with the sort of people the religious establishment designated 'sinners'. He even told the temple authorities that tax collectors and prostitutes were going into the kingdom of God ahead of them.

Within western culture our impression of 'sin' has been heavily influenced by the biblical story of Adam and Eve in the Garden of Eden, and the notorious 'forbidden fruit'. Even if we are not religious or particularly familiar with the story, some sense of its symbolism filters into our consciousness and colours our perception. But have we got the story right? Or could it be saying something quite different to what is generally thought?

The first thing to note is that, in literary terms, the story of the Garden of Eden belongs to the category of myth. We were never meant to read it literally or factually, though many people still do. Myths are like poetry in narrative form. They playfully explore the truths and mysteries of life, death and the universe: things that can never finally be translated into factual language. Myths are works of art, and like any work of art – any poem, story or picture – they invite different readings, different understandings.

According to the story, our mythical ancestors Adam and Eve were created by God and placed in a paradise of innocent perfection. They were told that they could eat as much as they wished from the Tree of Life in the middle of the garden, but never from the Tree of the Knowledge of Good and Evil. God told them that on the day they ate from that tree they would surely die.

It's hard not to be suspicious here. Everyone knows that if you place something enticing in front of a person, then tell him or her not to touch it, they immediately want to get their hands on it. Does God not understand curiosity? Was it a tease, or an example of reverse psychology? Did God in fact intend them to eat the fruit?

Either way, when the serpent tempted Eve she went ahead and ate the fruit, then persuaded Adam to have some too. Afterwards, the couple realised for the first time that they were naked, so covered their bodies. Seeing what they had done, God then caused them to leave the Garden of Eden forever.

From this point on, the woman would experience pain in childbirth and motherhood, God said, and the man would have to work for a living, earning his bread by the sweat of his brow. Also, both of them would live in dread of dying, and finally return to the dust from which they came.

Christians generally read Genesis 3 as a straightforward account of how sin entered the world, as a story of disobedience and punishment leading to the 'fall' of humanity and of all creation. Augustine, the early Church Father who massively influenced the shape of western Christianity, believed that as a result of Adam and Eve's action, sin became transmitted sexually through the human race so that all are infected with it, and all stand under the same judgement as Adam and Eve.[*]

Even as a child this story bothered me. Well, not so much the story, as the interpretation I was given. It seemed so intolerably unfair that one mistake should have such diabolical fallout for Adam and Eve, worse still that we

---

[*] Many biblical scholars disagree. For example, Professor of Old Testament Walter Brueggemann argues that nothing could be more remote from the narrative than the idea of 'the fall'. And Jewish theologians reject entirely the ideas of a 'fall' and original sin.

should all be dragged into their offence and damned along with them. I still remember the moment when the ghastly thought struck me that my beautiful, newly born little cousin who I adored was a condemned sinner, even though he hadn't done a single thing wrong. And it makes no more sense to me now than it did then.

But what if we read the passage with different eyes? What if we stop reading it through the lens of popular assumption and allow it to speak in a different way? What if it isn't an account of punishment for one monumental mistake, but a fable-like wisdom story about humans graduating, evolving from the relatively uncomplicated existence of animal innocence to the messy experience of moral responsibility? What if Adam and Eve didn't fall? What if they were pushed – by a God-given compulsion of nature? What if the voice of God in the story is a poignant warning about what lies ahead for a more highly evolved species rather than a straight-faced prohibition? What, in short, if we read the story with irony instead of literalism, with a grin rather than a grimace, as wisdom instead of dogma?

The 'judgements' that resulted from Adam and Eve eating the fruit can in fact be read as ambiguous blessings. Yes, the pain of childbirth is devastating, and something any woman would gladly skip over; yet isn't there something magnificent about the fact that we are born into this world through pain and suffering and yet we are thought to be worth all that and more? As for work, yes, it can be tough and stressful, and we may all grumble about it from time to time, but who wants a world where everything is on a plate, where there is no sweaty satisfaction from a task well done, no sitting down with a well-earned cold beer after a hard day? And who wants to live forever, anyway?

Hard work, sexual intimacy, parenthood, a sense of mortality, the knowledge of good and evil – aren't these the sort of things that make humans different to other creatures in a positive way? They present challenges and demands, and bring anxieties, yes, but they are also the source of imagination, creativity, rewarding struggle and achievement.

Rabbi Harold Kushner offers a magnificent version of how the story in Genesis might have ended, had Eve not had the courage to lead her husband into the brave new world of moral demands and ethical decisions.

So the woman saw that the tree was good to eat and a delight to the eye, and the serpent said to her, 'Eat of it, for when you eat of it, you will be as wise as God.' But the woman said, 'No, God has commanded us not to eat of it, and I will not disobey God.'

Did they fall, or were they pushed?

And God called to the man and the woman and said to them, 'Because you have hearkened to my word and not disobeyed my command, I shall reward you greatly.' To the man he said, 'You will never have to work again. Spend all your days in idle contentment, with food growing all around you.' To the woman, he said, 'You will bear children without pain and you will raise them without pain. They will need nothing from you. Children will not cry when their parents die, and parents will not cry when their children die.' To both of them he said, 'For the rest of your lives, you will have full bellies and contented smiles. You will never cry and you will never laugh. You will never long for something you don't have, and you will never receive something you always wanted.' And the man and the woman grew old together in the garden, eating daily from the Tree of Life and having children. And the grass grew high around the Tree of Knowledge of Good and Evil until it disappeared from view, for there was no one to tend it.*

---

* Quoted from Harold S. Kushner, *How Good Do We Have To Be?* (Little, Brown and Company, 1996), which also gives a more detailed alternative exposition of Genesis chapter 3.

Taking everything into account, how could we possibly imagine that eating from the Tree of Knowledge was a bad thing; surely, it was an act of bravery and liberation. Yes, of course there are consequences to having moral choice, but if the alternative is to live forever in innocence, driven simply by ethically neutral reflexes, then I know which world I prefer to inhabit.

A grown-up kind of God could not possibly wish for human beings to remain in paradise, in a state of innocence without knowledge of good and evil. He or she would be a control freak who wants playthings, not a God of love and integrity who looks for some level of mutuality with authentic people.

In order for humans to be human – people who make messes yet who also create beauty and goodness – the fruit *had* to be eaten. It was essential for us to have knowledge of good and evil. The story of Eden is not about paradise lost but paradise outgrown, not about the origin of sin but the birth of conscience and moral responsibility. It points to a grown-up God with growing-up humans.

Nevertheless, if we are to live as grown-ups, as moral beings in a moral universe, we cannot avoid the reality that we do indeed mess up – quite a lot. We are given freedom but we don't always use it wisely or correctly. However, the real problem is not that we mess up, but that we then try to shift the blame elsewhere, that we shirk responsibility for our sin.

Sin is a loaded term, which is why I barely use it. Yet we need 'sin' or something like it; we need a way to symbolise the reality of human imperfection and brokenness. Paul Tillich suggests that we think of sin as *separation*; i.e. to be in a state of sin is to be in a state of separation or estrangement. This separation surfaces in three ways, Tillich maintains: separation from neighbour, separation from our own deeper self, and separation from the Ground of our Being, which is God.

Looking at it from a slightly different viewpoint, sin is basically the absence of love. Whatever we can possibly call sin is the result of an absence of love. Love creates integration and wholeness; sin results in disintegration and brokenness.

Jesus said that the entire sum of religion could be summed up in these two commandments: to love God with all one's heart, soul and mind, and to love one's neighbour as one's self. Love is true religion in a nutshell. The rest is window-dressing.

Salvation is another word I tend to avoid, not because I don't like it, but because it has been hijacked in popular Christian lexis to mean 'going to heaven when we die'. Yet salvation has nothing to do with a pie in the sky afterlife. The word 'salvation' in English derives from a Latin word meaning 'wholeness' or 'healing'. Salvation is a here-and-now thing.

The story of Zacchaeus in the Gospels gives a good example of here-and-now salvation. He too was a tax collector, who made a fortune by defrauding people. But his wealth, accrued on the back of human misery, did not make him happy. He was alienated from his neighbours, hated for what he had become. More importantly, he was alienated from himself, from the person he most wanted to be. In order to treat fellow human beings with such contempt he had needed to cauterise his soul and conscience, to deny his natural sense of empathy, to become estranged from God, the ground of his existence.

When Zacchaeus heard that Jesus was visiting the neighbourhood, something stirred within him, and he knew he must see this man. Being short in stature, Zacchaeus famously climbed a tree on the road where he knew Jesus would travel. Jesus looked up and saw him hiding in the tree, and told him to come down. He then visited Zacchaeus' house for a drink and a quiet chat. Overwhelmed by the presence of one who was so totally whole and integrated, Zacchaeus gave half of his possessions to the poor, and repaid those he had swindled with four times what he had taken from them. 'Today salvation has come to this house,' Jesus said.

For Zacchaeus salvation had nothing to do with going to heaven; it was completely down to earth. He rediscovered his soul when he took responsibility for who he had become.

Ron is a more recent example of someone who experienced a here-and-now kind of salvation. Ron was the dad of a good friend of ours. He was brought up in the 1930s in depression-racked New Zealand, and made to attend church three times on Sundays, as well as during the week. It was a pretty joyless form of religion – absolutely anything enjoyable was judged to be wrong.

As soon as he could, Ron chucked church in, and gradually found solace in the bottle. He grew to abhor religion and wouldn't be found anywhere near a church. However he eventually found his way to an Alcoholics Anonymous group, and through the Twelve Steps programme learned to take responsibility for who he was.

At the age of fifty-seven, to everyone's surprise, Ron started a new business, which ended up being greatly successful, and he ended up running Alcoholics Anonymous meetings all over West London. When he died, Ron's ragtag funeral was packed to the rafters with former alcoholics, people that he had helped – each with a story of salvation to tell.

Perfection is not required of us. Honesty and the willingness to own up to what we are: this is what is required. When we finally receive this, when we outgrow our hankering after flawlessness and know that we are broken sinners, then we can discover the priceless joy of grace – we are accepted, accepted by that which is greater than us, however we name it. We are accepted. We are accepted. And that is all.

7. I found God!

she was behind the sofa the whole time

God is not difficult to find; God is impossible to avoid.

Deepak Chopra

It was a cold and blustery Valentine's Day on the River Thames. The rain lashed down. A strong wind tossed the tiny craft on the incoming tide. A storm was brewing – quite literally. But nothing could dampen the spirits of Karen and Hannah, the vessel's two very special passengers. It was their big day, when they would pledge themselves to each other for life. And the enormous smiles that covered their faces beamed sunshine into that miserable February afternoon as they sailed towards the Greenwich Yacht Club where their civil partnership ceremony would take place.

Over one hundred people gazed excitedly out of the clubhouse windows as the pilot attempted to dock the boat at the small jetty below. Finally the couple clambered ashore in their gorgeous, very individual, hand-made white dresses. Cameras clicked as the waiting throng watched the grinning couple pick their way through puddles in the boatyard, huddled under a large umbrella.

Then, at last, to everyone's delight, the happy couple appeared in the building to process joyfully down the aisle to Ellie Goulding's version of the song 'How long will I love you?'

I have a lot of very satisfying days in my job, but this was definitely one of my favourites – conducting the civil partnership ceremony of two beautiful lovebirds on Valentine's Day. It's frustrating and stupid that I still can't conduct such a ceremony in a church, as a vicar. But nothing could detract from the joy of that day. And in the end, love will conquer discrimination and small-mindedness.

It is very unusual (unheard of, in my experience) for a

non-registrar to be allowed to conduct a civil partnership ceremony. I felt honoured on that score alone. But, of course, no mention of God is allowed at such an event; no religious references admitted. Even requests for songs like Leonard Cohen's 'Hallelujah' are customarily turned down. So I chuckled when the wonderful 'Eclectic Voices' choir that Hannah sings with belted out '*Sifuni mungu*', a song of praise to God in Swahili, based on the hymn 'All creatures of our God and King'. (I wonder if there is a Swahili version of Cohen's 'Hallelujah'!)

Of course, once the paper is signed and the registrar has left, you can do what you want, which we did. But even before that, it had been agreed that we could include in the ceremony a ritual I had previously used at a couple of very special weddings.

First, Karen and Hannah shared wine with each other to celebrate the greater sweetness they would experience by drinking from the cup of life together. Then, they exchanged a pinch of salt on the tongue to remember the bitter and unhappy times they would also share. Finally, they gave each other bread, symbolising their daily life together as a couple, which was then passed around the entire congregation, uniting us all in wishing them the very best.

There were many leaky eyes as the bread passed from hand to hand, but I couldn't help smiling at the irony that, not just Karen and Hannah, but the whole congregation shared a moment of 'communion' in an entirely secular ceremony; also that the happy couple drank wine from one of the church's silver chalices. God may not have been mentioned by name in that ceremony but she really was behind the sofa the whole time!

After a lifetime of seeking to know God better, the most important thing I have discovered is that we cannot *find* God. The notion of 'finding' God is in fact the most absurd idea on earth. God was never lost. And we were never lost to God. God is everywhere, named or unnamed, recognised or unrecognised, bidden or unbidden – *behind* the sofa, *under* the sofa, *on* the sofa and *within* the sofa.

Deepak Chopra says that if you can't find God in a rainbow, if you can't find God in a blade of grass, if you can't find God in the eyes of another being or in the smile of a child, you will not discover God in a book of religion. To which I would add, if you can't find God in two women (or men) committing themselves to undying love for each other, you need a bigger notion of who or what God is.

After the ceremony I gave a short talk which ended with a gentle spin on the words of St John, to say: 'God is friendship and those who live in friendship live in God and God lives in them.'* I can think of no better summary of everything I know and believe about God. For me, all the rest is embellishment, window-dressing.

Over the meal afterwards, at the bar, on the dance floor, and outside in the wind and rain puffing a cigar with the smokers, I found people eager to discuss what happened in the ceremony, and what I said in my talk. One person told me, 'You've helped me to see that God is all around me, that God may even be inside me.'

The impression we are often given is that we have to *do* something in order to find God: 'accept' Jesus, read the Bible, pray, go to church etc. However, there is nothing we have to do in order to find God but open our eyes. We already know God, we just don't necessarily use that name to describe her. God is part of all our lives. When we experience unconditional love from a friend, we experience God. When we sense the wondrous grace of another day dawning, we experience God. When we reach out to another person with compassion, when we resist an injustice, when we sacrifice our own comfort to make another person more comfortable, when we forgive until it hurts, we experience God. There is a magnet in each of us that repels hatred and injustice, and impels us towards

---

* 1 John 4:16 actually reads: 'God is love, and those who live in love live in God, and God lives in them.'

kindness, integrity and friendship. Inasmuch as we surrender to that magnetic force, rather than work against it, we connect with the presence of God within.

Joan Chittister, a wonderful Catholic nun whose writings constantly inspire me, says, 'Wherever I am, whatever my state of mind, God is the spirit within me, and the life in me. God is there for the taking. God is the air I breathe, and God is the path I take. God is the womb in which I live.'[*]

> The human spirit is the lamp of the Lord.
> *Proverbs 20:27*

This description of God differs radically from the vision of God we are often given: the 'man upstairs', the supernatural being 'out there' who created the world and occasionally intervenes in it. What Joan Chittister points to is a God who surrounds us, who is the breath in our lungs, the very basis of our existence, a God it is impossible to avoid even when we ignore her.

It isn't always admitted, but throughout history Christians have inevitably used the prevailing contemporary worldview to shape their beliefs and practices. It

---

[*] Joan Chittister, *In Search of Belief* (Redemptorist Publications, 1999).

cannot be avoided. There can be no notion of the Christian gospel, no vision of God, no interpretation of the Bible that is not significantly influenced by the surrounding culture and the understanding it has of the world. We define our faith in conjunction with, *or over against*, the ideas of the day.

In biblical times, the prevailing worldview envisaged a three-tier universe in which the earth was central, with heaven above, and hell (or the grave) beneath. In that scheme of things, it seemed natural to envisage God as the great king of the universe, or as a cosmic judge, or as a patriarchal father-figure in the heavens 'looking down' on earth, 'watching over' us, intervening whenever he saw fit.

Because this image of God is embedded in the biblical text, it has become the accepted way to picture God. Even today, it still forms the basis of most Christians' notion of who or what God is, as well as the basis for most atheists' rejection of God. But times have changed. We see the world and the universe very differently, and we can see God differently too.

In our scientific, ecological age the emphasis is on interconnectedness. The hierarchical picture that once existed, of God ruling everything from heaven, and man as God's earthly viceroy having headship over the woman and ruling over the creatures of earth, is long gone, thank goodness (even though we still live with some of the aftermath of that vision).

So it is time to dig deeper into our tradition for different symbols and images of divinity, which are more consonant with the new story of the universe, the story of evolutionary development and cosmic interconnectedness. Instead of a God directing the world from the outside, we need to discover the everywhere God: the God who is in all, with all, and operating in all: the God who is the ground of being, who is existence itself.

While the dominant vision of God within Christian tradition is the idea of a supernatural, humanlike being 'out there' who occasionally intervenes in the world, another vision does exist, which sees God as the all-encompassing Spirit in whom everything exists. The universe is not separate from God, but *in* God. Like a fish living and moving and having its entire existence within a vast ocean, we, and all that is, exist within God.

Throughout the Bible, Spirit is used to refer to God's all-pervading presence in creation. The word 'spirit' in Hebrew is a feminine noun meaning wind or breath, which conjures up lots of ideas and images. Both wind and breath are invisible yet obviously real. We cannot see wind but we can see and feel its effects. When it blows it surrounds us; we are engulfed by it and feel its force. Breath is the same as wind but in the body. We cannot see it, yet without it we would die.

If we think of God as Spirit, then, like the air, God is all around us and within us. We cannot escape God, because we breathe God constantly. God is the breath in our lungs and the oxygen of our soul. I think of breathing as a sacred act, a prayer without words, a spiritual practice. Every breath is a gracious gift of life. When I sit calmly and become aware of my breathing, I cannot help but feel gratitude, but I also feel peace.

Breathing is the most primitive form of prayer we have. Nothing is more soothing and relaxing than quiet, conscious breathing. It calms fears and discharges panic. It grounds us in the body, re-centres the mind and spirit, and helps us to get the world in perspective.

Sometimes when I have a church full of non-church-goers, gathered for a baptism or a wedding, I invite them to take a few moments of quiet, to place their feet on the floor, then breathe and focus on the young child or the couple. After a short while I ask them to open their eyes, then tell them that they have just prayed. People with no particular religious beliefs have told me that they had no idea that praying was that easy. One woman said, 'I'm going to do that every day.' Conscious breathing is one of the simplest and most effective ways of connecting us to the life force, which is God. That is how close God is: as near to us as our breath.

Many people who will never come near a church, who do not think of themselves as even remotely religious, experience an occasional feeling of ecstatic oneness with the mystery behind everything. For example, when gazing into the heavens at night, or standing in the midst of an open space in the country and feeling that they are a very tiny part of something vast and great. This also is a form of prayer.

> *I believe in mystery and, frankly, I sometimes face this mystery with great fear. In other words, I think that there are many things in the universe that we cannot perceive or penetrate, and that also we experience some of the most beautiful things in life only in a very primitive form. Only in relation to these mysteries do I consider myself to be a religious man.*
>
> *Albert Einstein*

Jean came from a particularly non-religious background. When we met to discuss her sister's funeral she told me how she had been sucked into a life of drug-taking and prostitution in the King's Cross area of London. She had fled home as a young teenager to escape the abuse of her father, and slept rough. Her 'knight in shining armour' turned out to be a pimp. Drugs helped for a while, but things got worse, until one night she found a back entrance into a tall building in Central London and climbed the fire escape stairs until she made her way onto the roof with a bottle of whisky and some pills.

Lying on top of the building, she gazed into the sky and saw stars. Thousands of stars. 'I'd never done that since I was a little girl,' she said. 'I stared and stared, and thought how perfect and how peaceful it all looked – so different to my sick life. And that's when I decided not to kill myself. I suddenly felt as if I was in this massive womb about to be born. Something was looking after me.'

Jean wasn't formally religious; she didn't go to church or claim to be a Christian, but when I suggested it to her, she readily recognised that the 'something' looking after her was God. By the time we met, she had been in recovery from drink and drugs for thirteen years, and she now works with a team going out on the streets befriending girls who live like she once did, offering them support and counselling. She didn't have a religious conversion, as such, yet her life was transformed by discovering that she wasn't alone in the world; that God was behind her sofa the whole time.

I have sometimes had a similar experience to Jean in the midst of crowds of people. At a rock concert, or a football match, or even walking through central London I have sensed a sudden oneness with people in their joy and sorrow. Something connects us deep down, and I think that 'something' is God, the all-encompassing Spirit of life. If we sense this it will not only be personally transforming, it will also transform our relationships, our society, our world.

This was the realisation that dawned on Thomas Merton, the Trappist monk, when he stood in the midst of the busy shopping area of Louisville, Kentucky. He suddenly felt overwhelmed with the realisation that he loved all the people he saw; that even though they were all strangers, something bound them together. 'It is a glorious destiny to be a member of the human race,' he thought. 'There is no way of telling people that they are walking around shining like the sun.' In that moment he saw the secret of people's hearts – to that place deep down where neither sin nor desire can reach, the core of their reality, the person each one is in God's eyes. And he longed to show them who they really were. 'If only we could see each other that way all of the time', Merton writes. 'There would be no more war, no more hatred, no more cruelty, no more greed.'

I recall a similar experience when I was nineteen, working as a printer in Liverpool. My printing machine stood by a window on the second floor looking out on a bustling city centre street. And I recall standing, gazing out of the window one day as the machine churned out five thousand shoebox labels, and watching the people as they passed by. In a mysterious moment, I sensed the burdens they were carrying – the fears and anxieties, the guilt and disappointment, the sadness and loss – and I wanted to open the window and tell them that God was all around them, that they were not alone but loved, held, supported. Fortunately, I resisted the compulsion to bellow my message from the window; yet the sense of an enormous loving presence surrounding people, binding us together in our common humanity, has never left me. It is the basis of everything I am and do.

Church buildings are often referred to as 'the house of God', but the whole earth, the entire universe, is filled with God's presence. We do not need to go to any special place, arouse any special state of mind, listen to the teachings of any particular teacher or religion in order to discover God. We simply need to wake up to what is already there.

There is a story in the Old Testament about the prophet Elijah in a state of utter despair, trying to find God. First he looked for God in a mighty wind, then in an earth-quake, and then in a fire. Eventually there was a sound of sheer silence. And it was in the silence that Elijah found God, speaking to him in a quiet voice – behind the sofa the whole time.

8. Tea and biscuits religion

it's about making friends, for God's sake

We may have different religions, different languages, different coloured skin, but we all belong to one human race.

Kofi Anan

I am a keen supporter of 'tea and biscuits religion', the subversive art of godly civility.

A dramatic example of this appeared in the aftermath of the brutal killing of Drummer Lee Rigby in Woolwich in May 2013. The attack was ruthless and insane. Two self-proclaimed 'soldiers of Allah' drove a car into the twenty-five-year-old fusilier outside his South London army barracks, and then hacked him to death, shouting 'Allahu Akbar' (God is great).

Within a week of the killing, over two hundred Islamophobic incidents were reported across the country (multitudes more went unreported), including attacks on mosques and widespread verbal and physical assaults on Muslims. An Islamic centre close to where I live in North London was destroyed by fire. And a female Muslim friend told me how she was spat on as she walked down the street and had her hijab torn from her head.

Yet when a far-right group targeted a mosque in York for an anti-Islamic demonstration, representatives of the local Muslim community responded with spectacular civility, inviting the demonstrators into the mosque for a nice cup of tea and a custard cream, followed by an impromptu game of football.

I laughed out loud with delight when I heard news of this.

Mohammed el-Gomati, a lecturer at the University of York and an elder at the mosque, commented,

> There is the possibility of having dialogue ... Who knows, perhaps the EDL [the far-right English

Defence League] will invite us to an event and the Muslim community will be generous in accepting that invitation ... If people sat down and talked, they may come to common, shared ground rather than shouting from a distance and not hearing what the other person is saying.

The Archbishop of York, John Sentamu, chuckled as only he can, describing the initiative as fantastic: 'Tea, biscuits and football are a great and typically Yorkshire combination when it comes to disarming hostile and extremist views,' he said.

A local politician spoke of the gesture as a proud moment for the city, commenting, 'I don't think I'll ever forget the day that the York Mosque tackled anger and hatred with peace and warmth – and I won't forget the sight of a Muslim offering a protester tea and biscuits with absolute sincerity.'

I am a priest. Every week I dispense bread and wine to people in the Eucharist. But I can't imagine a more effective sacrament of divine grace than tea and custard creams served in a mosque with kindness and magnanimity. I only wish I had been there to partake of such holy 'communion'.

The world has had its fill of religious hatred and conflict. It is time for people of good faith in every tradition to affirm kindness as a central feature of religious life: not wishy-washy niceness, but big-hearted, brave benevolence infused with wisdom and supported by tenacity. The world's faiths will never achieve unity of belief (nor should they), but we must at all costs pursue unity of heart and purpose. We must be friends, for God's sake.

Every month I make the short pilgrimage to the end of the District Line on the London Underground to take part in an interfaith forum. I count it as a spiritual practice. We meet in the Coopers Company and Coborn School in Upminster, which has the spectacularly appropriate motto, 'Love as Brethren: Encourage Learning'. The regular panel consists of an ordained Buddhist, a Muslim imam, a Reform Jew and me. Occasionally, a Shamanic Pagan joins us. In the audience we have a delightful mix of representatives of local faith communities and sixth-form students from the school.

After a short presentation from each speaker, we adjourn for 'interfaith sandwiches' and conversation, and then reconvene, inviting the whole gathering to contribute to the discussion. It's tea and biscuits religion, all right: passionate faith debated in a civil manner, with mutual respect, good-hearted disagreement, and not infrequent bouts of laughter.

Perhaps more than anything else, I enjoy the contributions from the students. We try to link the discussion topics with their religious education curriculum, as an added incentive for them to take part, which they mostly do. I only wish that I had been exposed to such generous interfaith discussion as a young person instead of growing up in Christian isolation, being told that everyone else would go to hell.

My engagement with interfaith dialogue developed over some years, but a crucial point was reached during a planning meeting for a large Christian event where I was invited to be one of three speakers in a seminar looking at different faiths. Each of us was designated twenty minutes to talk about Islam, Hinduism or Buddhism. I was allocated Buddhism.

We were handed a set of notes to work from. Up to that point, I was under the impression that the object of the seminar was education. But reading through the notes I rapidly realised that it was an exercise in propaganda, not education, designed simply to contrast the 'truth' of Christianity with the error of the other faiths. 'I can't possibly do this,' I protested; 'it's a stitch-up. If someone wrote this sort of stuff about Christianity we would be outraged, and rightly so.'

Predictably, my intervention did not go down well. And when I suggested an alternative strategy: that we set aside the notes and invite some real Muslims, Hindus and Buddhists to join us for a proper discussion about the different faiths, there were grim looks all around. After a pause, the chair of the meeting politely submitted that perhaps this seminar wasn't for me. What a relief! Yet I went home exhilarated by the experience, and convinced that I needed to seek out more face-to-face interaction with people of other religious traditions.

Now, twenty-five years later, I have many friends in other faith communities who I consider fellow travellers in the quest for truth and spiritual enlightenment. We are not all the same. We follow different religious paths; hold different beliefs. Yet we share a common humanity, which is far more fundamental than our religious differences. And I believe that as we, each in our own way, seek to become better human beings, we instinctively move towards the heart of what it is that we all most deeply believe in, yet name differently.

The philosopher Jacob Needleman tells a story about a very high mountain, the top of which represents being with God. Because the mountain is so high, it needs a massive base, traversing many cultures and climate zones. People have traditions about how to climb the mountain, depending on where they are situated around it. In tropical climates they set out in short pants, a safari helmet and mosquito netting. In arctic climates they wear a snow parka, goggles and boots to climb the mountain.

When the people from the tropical climates get about halfway up, they start to feel the cold and need to go back to get a sweater. When the people from the colder climates get halfway up, they have to shed their outer clothing because it feels too warm. However, when the climbers get to the top – you've guessed it – they end up dressed pretty much the same way. The problem, says Needleman, is when people walk around the base of the mountain and argue about how to dress.

Needleman is not the first to observe that religious communities function like separate cultures, each with its own language, its own customs and rituals, its own notions of who or what God is. But whereas in the past they tended to exist in quite different geographical regions of the globe, today the world's religions live cheek by jowl in the same town and city, the same neighbourhood. And this throws up obvious questions, which are difficult to avoid. Is it still possible to believe that our religion alone offers access to God? What is the real difference between the faiths? Does the same God listen to everyone when they pray? How should the faith communities cooperate to create a better world?

The Jewish writer Chaim Potok grapples with precisely these sorts of questions in his novel *The Book of Lights*. The central character, a rabbinical student called Gershon Loran, is the product of a parochial New York Jewish upbringing, where he was taught that Judaism had made a fundamental difference to the world. But his preconceptions were challenged while serving in Korea and Japan at the end of the Korean War. Realising that there were massive sections of the world where Judaism had played no part, he began to see his faith, his people and himself in a new light.

The novel isn't autobiographical but Potok draws inspiration from his own experience as an army chaplain in Korea and Japan. He writes:

> *I came into that experience with a very neat coherent picture of what I was as an American and what I was as a Jew. All that neat, antique coherence came undone in the fifteen and a half months that I spent in that part of the world. I remember when I was very, very young, being taught by my father and my teachers that paganism was intrinsically an abomination. I came to Japan and to Korea and saw pagan loveliness I never dreamed I could see. The sheer beauty of that pagan world overwhelmed me. Although it was manmade*

loveliness, its beauty was created by the human hand
for the purposes of worship. I learned to appreciate
*the loveliness of God's world in a pagan land.**

There is a scene in the book where the young rabbi and his companion visit a shrine in Japan, maybe Buddhist or Shinto, where they witness a man standing before the altar, hands pressed together, eyes closed, rocking slightly, engaged in prayer. The rabbi turns to his friend and says, 'Do you think our God is listening to him, John?'

'I don't know . . . I never thought of it,' John replies.

'Neither did I until now. If He's not listening, why not? If He is listening, then – well, what are we all about, John?'

I recall having a very similar thought in a Sikh temple many years ago. Impressed with the devotion of the people, I found it impossible to imagine that the God I believed in would not listen to their prayers too. But that led to a further, more searching question: Is 'my God' also 'their God'? And if so, what does that say about my faith and my own special relationship with God?

The issue of religious difference evokes a variety of responses, which can be distilled into three basic answers

---

* Chaim Potok, *The Book of Lights* (Alfred A. Knopf, 1981).

to the question: is our God listening to the prayers of people of other faiths?

1. Our God is not listening to those of other faiths

This is the voice of religious fundamentalism, echoes of which can be heard in all the world's faith communities. It insists that our tradition and ours alone – our scriptures, our worldview, our encounter with God – represents the one and only truth. All the rest are wrong.

Those who take this approach appear to have disturbing resilience against the diabolical horror of a God that could write off whole swathes of humanity because people were born in the 'wrong' place or to the 'wrong' family. They have no qualms in speaking about 'our God', or in crudely dividing the world between 'us' and 'them', 'believers' and 'unbelievers', the 'saved' and the 'unsaved', those who will go to heaven and the rest who will go to hell.

I know many Christians who hold this view or something very close to it, some of whom frequently confront me in public, or send me (sometimes angry) messages condemning what they see as my 'liberal' views on the Bible, sexuality and other religions. However I have occasionally encountered the same attitude in interfaith forums, like the time when an enthusiastic young Muslim told me that I faced hellfire if I refused to believe the one and only truth which is Islam.

While I find myself deeply impatient with this *exclusivist* approach to religion, I remind myself that it is what I grew up with and took for granted for many years. Nevertheless, I now see it as regressive and irrational, and only sustainable within a closed mind-set that ignores the obvious critical questions it raises.

2. Our God is listening, but it is our God, as we understand God, who does the listening

I suspect that many, perhaps most, non-fundamentalist Christians instinctively answer the question this way, even when they haven't consciously thought it through. For such people, the idea that God callously ignores the prayers and aspirations of people of other faiths or, worse still, ultimately condemns them to hell for not following the Christian way, is abhorrent.

C.S. Lewis articulates this *inclusivist* slant on religion when he states, 'I think that every prayer which is sincerely made even to a false god . . . is accepted by the true God and that Christ saves many who do not think they know him.' Similarly, the Catholic theologian Karl Rahner wrote positively about the possibility of salvation outside Christianity. He talked about 'anonymous Christians', and envisaged the great religions of the world being covered by God's grace, regardless of their beliefs and practices.

The inclusivist approach has much to be said for it, compared with the mean-spiritedness of exclusivism. Finding it in the writings of C.S. Lewis probably kept me from abandoning faith altogether, at one stage. That said, it readily slips into a form of condescension, based on the assumption that there can be only one language to speak of God, which is ours. The self-understanding of people in other faiths has no validity in and of itself; our faith represents the ultimate norm.

3. Yes, of course God listens to everyone. But ultimately, there is no 'our God'. God is a Reality that cannot be encompassed by any one religious tradition, including our own

This is the response of people who believe that truth is not the sole possession of any one tradition or community. *Pluralism* maintains that every image or notion of God, including our own, is limited and relative, that God transcends our idea of God. No single faith tradition can therefore claim to have the exclusive truth about God, or exclusive access to God.

I think of religious traditions, including my own, as

windows on a Reality that is far too great to be seen from any one perspective. The windows represent vantage points, perceptions of God that may be real and valid yet which are at best partial and miniscule compared with the thing itself.

It is perfectly possible to maintain fully the integrity of one's own faith while accepting the prospect of God being revealed in other ways within other faith communities. We need a policy therefore of 'dialogue with steadfastness' – a commitment to listen to others, and learn from them, while remaining rooted in our own tradition.

This, of course, is what I experience every month with my colleagues in our interfaith forum. If I see Christ as the way, the truth and the life, there is no reason why I cannot also accept that there are other ways, other truths, other life from the Torah, the Qur'an, or the Eightfold Path of the Buddha. These are not my tradition, yet I can happily affirm their validity without giving up my commitment to the way of Christ.

If we think of different religious faiths as linguistic traditions, as different faith languages to describe the divine, then it is possible to recognise interfaith dialogue as an effort to gain at least a basic grasp of other religious languages. And maybe this can help us to avoid being like the proverbial Englishman abroad who always expects people to speak English.

Certainly, dialogue helps us to recognise the great commonalities embedded in our traditions, which can contribute towards creating a better world. Based on this assumption, Hans Kung and others produced a statement of a 'global ethic', which representatives of all the world's faiths have signed up to: a commitment to non-violence, justice, truthfulness and partnership between men and women.

Kung argues that the values we need today are rooted in all the great religious and philosophical traditions of humankind. We don't need to invent them, but we do need to be made aware of them again; they must be lived out and handed on. So there is need for:

- **A dialogue of religions and cultures**, especially a knowledge of common features in ethics.
- **An education in values which transcends cultures**. Children, too, need to learn that peaceful coexistence at all levels depends on observing elementary rules. No society can function without a foundation of values which binds it together.
- **Ethical and intercultural competence in business**. More than ever, enterprises competing internationally need norms which transcend cultures.

- **International policies anchored in law and ethics:** understanding, cooperation and integration instead of military confrontation.

Our post-9/11 world needs a global ethic based on Kung's motto: 'No peace among the nations without peace among religions. No peace among the religions without dialogue.' In a world torn apart by war, violence and terrorism, much of which seems inextricably tied up with religion, we desperately need people of good faith across the world's religions, working together for the common good.

It's not rocket science. It's about making friends for God's sake. It's about more tea and biscuits religion, the subversive art of godly civility.

9 'Just a shot like the rest of us'

In 2012...

9. 'Just a slob like one of us?'*

why I am still a Jesus freak

Each one of them is Jesus in disguise.

Mother Teresa

In 2010, Sir Elton John sparked outrage among Christians by suggesting that Jesus was gay. He told the American magazine *Parade*:

---

* This is a line from Joan Osborne's song 'One of us'.

I think Jesus was a compassionate, super-intelligent gay man who understood human problems. On the cross, he forgave the people who crucified him. Jesus wanted us to be loving and forgiving. I don't know what makes people so cruel. Try being a gay woman in the Middle East – you're as good as dead.

Conservative churchgoers were incensed by this; the rock star received a barrage of letters, emails and tweets accusing him of blasphemy, and telling him that he was an evil sinner, doomed to hell. There were even death threats. The Catholic League, America's largest Catholic civil rights organisation, issued a bulletin stating: 'to call Jesus a homosexual is to label him a sexual deviant'. It went on to propose that someone should 'straighten' Elton John out! (Good luck with that one, I say.)

In Britain, the response was more muted. A spokesman for the Church of England said: 'Sir Elton's reflection that Jesus calls us all to love and forgive is one shared by all Christians, but insights into aspects of the historic person of Jesus are perhaps best left to the academics.' Admirable Anglican restraint we might think, if somewhat patronising. But actually, it completely misses the real point behind this hullabaloo, which is not about historical accuracy but about identity and inclusion: Jesus belongs to LGBT people too.

Elton John wasn't saying anything disparaging about Jesus; quite the reverse. He was simply saying that this is what Jesus symbolises to him as a gay man: compassion and forgiveness in the face of cruelty and hatred. In a subsequent interview he said:

> *I think everyone's individual faith is their own business. And I do believe in Jesus, and I do believe he was a compassionate person. And I see him from my point of view, and that's just my point of view, as a compassionate gay person – someone who was persecuted, someone who forgave people . . . That's how I see him. I'm not saying, 'That's how he definitely was.'*

Was Jesus gay? I haven't the faintest clue. And actually, I don't give a hoot. Certainly, I recognise the Spirit of Christ among gay people in precisely the same way that I do among straight people. I see no difference. So why on earth should it matter?

I have not the slightest shadow of a doubt that if the Jesus in the Gospels were living today he would incorporate LGBT people among his followers; he would be a vociferous advocate of gay rights. I can hear him telling a story about the good transsexual who fought off a mugger attacking an old man while a vicar hurried by on the other side of the street. I can imagine him admonishing his narrow-minded disciples when they tried to stop a lesbian couple from bringing their child to him for a blessing.

On one occasion in John's Gospel when some of Jesus' critics wanted to hurl abuse at him, they told him, 'You are a Samaritan and have a demon?'[*] Jesus wasn't a Samaritan; no one imagined that he was. But his critics used the name of their sworn enemies as a racist expletive to demean him. But Jesus simply replied, 'I do not have a demon.' To have also denied being a Samaritan would have been to collude with their bigotry, which he refused to do. In today's world, they may have said, 'You're a fag and a pervert', to which he would have responded, 'I am not a pervert.'

The fact is, wittingly or unwittingly, Elton John opened up a profound and urgent theological question, which is also intensely practical: 'Who is Jesus Christ for us today?' Dietrich Bonhoeffer, the German theologian and opponent of the Nazis, posed this question just before the end of the war as he waited in a Nazi prison to be executed. Sensing that the world was changing, Bonhoeffer felt that conventional notions of Christ were no longer enough. 'What is bothering me incessantly', he wrote, 'is the

---

[*] John 8:48.

question what Christianity really is, or indeed who Christ really is, for us today.'

In the past, Christ has been identified with a male-dominated, white, middle-class establishment that imposed its values, attitudes and prejudices on society, but today we must ask: who is Jesus Christ for women still waiting for full equality with men? Who is Jesus Christ for LGBT people daring at last to speak their name? Who is Jesus Christ for people of colour living in a Christian culture that assumes he was white? Who is Jesus Christ for the poor and powerless, when the church is rich and influential? Who is Jesus Christ for immigrants, sex workers, rock singers, shelf fillers or domestic cleaners? Who is Jesus Christ for a woman in Africa dying of AIDS, for a man slowly departing this world in a care home in North London?

The way we picture Jesus is critical to our understanding of the Christian faith: it shapes our notion of what Christianity is, and can also make it credible or incredible. Frankly, I would probably have jumped ship on the whole thing long ago were it not for the figure of Jesus and what that means to me. When there is so much that wearies and repels me about the church and Christianity, I find myself perpetually re-converted by Jesus and what he represents to me.

In the film *Hannah and Her Sisters*, Woody Allen has one of the characters remark, 'If Jesus came back and saw what was being done in his name, he'd never stop throwing up.' My confidence that this is fundamentally true is a significant part of what keeps me on board.

Who, then, is Jesus Christ for us today? Despite vital and valiant efforts by biblical scholars to reconstruct him, the carpenter of Nazareth has now disappeared in the mists of time. No one can say with genuine authority, 'This is the real Jesus', because history will not get you that far. I certainly feel confident that the Jesus of the Gospels would be gobsmacked at many of the ways he has been represented by believers and non-believers alike over the centuries.

The Gospels in the New Testament provide our main picture of Jesus. Yet all four of these were written decades after his life, and were not composed as biographies or literal histories of Jesus, but rather as testimonies to what the early Christian communities came to believe about him in the light of the resurrection. They are a mixture of memory, metaphor and faith. This isn't to say that they are untrue; truth is not always the same as literal fact, as any lover of poetry, art or literature understands. However it does mean that we should know what we are reading, and how to make sense of it.

Marcus Borg, a New Testament scholar, emphasises the importance of distinguishing between the pre-Easter Jesus and the post-Easter Jesus.[*]

The pre-Easter Jesus is *Jesus before his death*: a Galilean Jew born around 4 BCE and executed by the Romans around the year 30 CE. This flesh-and-blood Jesus – the itinerant Jewish mystical teacher and healer who sided with sinners and outcasts against the religious establishment – is dead and gone; he no longer exists. This is not a denial of Easter, or of people's experience of the risen Christ, just a straightforward fact: the physical Jesus is now a figure of history.

The post-Easter Jesus, on the other hand, is *what Jesus became after his death*. This is the Jesus of Christian tradition and experience, often referred to as 'the Christ of faith', the Jesus who continued to be experienced by his followers after his death, and who is still experienced by Christians today. The post-Easter Jesus is the Jesus we encounter in the New Testament as a whole, and in the ecumenical creeds and church liturgy.

The Gospels represent a mixture of both the pre- and post-Easter Jesus; they present stories of a flesh-and-blood

---

[*] See for example Marcus Borg's *Meeting Jesus Again for the First Time: The Historical Jesus and the Contemporary Faith* (HarperOne, 1995).

Jesus together with his teaching, framed within the developing theological traditions in the early Christian community. Therefore, as Marcus Borg notes, the Gospels contain two voices: the voice of Jesus, and the voice of the early church. Discerning which is which is precisely the sort of question that preoccupies scholars pursuing the 'quest for the historical Jesus', the theological endeavour to create an authentic historical portrait of who Jesus was.

One of the big questions most curious followers of Jesus ask at some point is: how did Jesus see himself? To what extent did he think about himself as the church came to see him, i.e. as the Christ of creed and stained-glass window, as the only begotten Son of God, the second person of the Trinity, God made flesh and so forth?

The British New Testament scholar James Dunn argues that, while the term 'Son of God' barely crossed the lips of Jesus in the Gospels, he probably did see himself as God's son. Yet, surprisingly, this is not the same as thinking that he was divine, Dunn says. After centuries of Christian conditioning, we automatically assume that this is what 'son of God' implies, but at the time of Christ the phrase was a way of characterising someone who was thought to be commissioned by God, or highly favoured by God, and not divine. And in terms of Jesus' own self-awareness, all we can talk about with confidence, Dunn states, is of his sense of intimate sonship to God as Father, whose nearest parallel would place him among the righteous of the Wisdom literature or identify him as an esteemed charismatic rabbi.

The idea that Jesus saw himself as the second person in the Trinity (the 'Son' in 'Father, Son and Holy Spirit') is anachronistic and entirely incongruous with the religious environment Jesus lived in. A trinitarian notion of God was utterly foreign to the Jewish mentality of Christ's time, as it is today. The Christian apologist Tertullian first used the term 'trinity' in the early third century, and the doctrine of the Holy Trinity was not established until the First Council of Nicaea in 325 CE, which is when the church officially declared Jesus to be divine and called him God.

It is abundantly clear from Matthew's, Mark's and Luke's Gospels, that Jesus himself avoided grand titles and labels. His preferred way of speaking about himself was as 'the son of man', a term which in his own language and culture denoted a human being *in contrast to* deity, and with special reference to human weakness and frailty – 'I'm only human' in today's vernacular.

The phrase 'the son of man', which is not a gendered term (it better translates as 'the human being'), appears eighty-two times in the Gospels, but only ever on the lips of Jesus, leading to an overwhelming consensus that this was a strong element in the speech of the original Jesus. Yet, interestingly, unlike 'son of God', which has been an essential element of Christian creeds from the start, the notion of Jesus as 'the son of man' or 'the human being' never appears in any creed, or as an article of faith in Christianity.

The church traditionally holds that Jesus was both human and divine, but the concentration on 'son of God' to the exclusion of 'son of man' has added to an over-whelming emphasis on his divinity. And in much popular Christian spirituality this has led to a general tendency to see Jesus as a God-Man and not a real human being.

For me, as a Christian, Jesus is the definitive revelation of God. I automatically gauge every other claim concerning the nature of divinity by what I see of Jesus in the Gospels and what I understand of him in my experience. Jesus is my spiritual magnetic north, my guiding star, and the constant focus of my attention. I am an unashamed Jesus freak.

However, I am far more interested in trying to follow the way of Jesus than in standing around admiring him. One of the most emasculating processes in the history of the Christian gospel is the transformation of the radical Jesus, who called people to take up their cross and follow him, into the institutional, stained-glass Christ-figure passively worshipped and revered. Our real goal should be to recapture the original impulse of Jesus, the Spirit that drove him to be who he was, to do what he did.

I have long been inspired and influenced by the writing of the now sadly departed Walter Wink, the American professor of biblical interpretation. In a book devoted entirely to exploring the phrase 'the son of man' or 'the human being', Wink's main aim is to make Christianity more plausible in the modern world; in effect, to explore who Jesus Christ is for us today.

Abandoning ecclesiastical gobbledegook about the metaphysical nature of Christ's divinity, Wink argues for a lean and pared-back Christianity, which isn't offering the world creeds, dogmas, doctrines, liturgies and devotions, but simply Jesus, the human being who reveals God by revealing what humanity can look like.

What I and others similarly inclined are trying to do is to move Christianity in a more humane direction. For that task we seek a Jesus who is not the omnipotent God in a man-suit, but someone like us, who looked for God at the center of his life and called the world to join him.*

---

* Walter Wink, *The Human Being: Jesus and the Enigma of the Son of God* (Fortress Press, 2002).

Incarnation (the notion that God becomes a human being and takes human form) is one of the most compelling aspects of Christianity. However, when incarnation is 'frozen' to become a one-off event in the past with the original coming of Jesus, we overlook or diminish the myriad ways that God becomes flesh and blood in the world every single day.

The problem, as I see it, is that incarnation is too often embedded in an outmoded vision of the 'man upstairs' sort of God who chose to visit the world as a miraculous, super-human hybrid: 'an omnipotent God in a man-suit', as Walter Wink puts it. Jesus in this scenario can never be one of us, a proper human being teaching us how to be fully human.

But when we begin to think about God as the divine presence in all things, the very Ground of our Being, the breath of life in all that lives, then incarnation is a constant reality all around, not a one-off event in history. God is no longer a visitor from somewhere 'far beyond the blue', but the source of life and energy in all that exists.

As Michael Dowd, an eco-theologian, says: 'at no point in time during the past four and a half billion years, the age of our solar system, did anyone come from outside and put anything on the planet. God is the inner dynamic guiding the process, the living reality revealed in and through creation . . ."* The whole point of Jesus' life is that a human being – a 'slob like one of us' – lived in such a way that people around him believed that they beheld the divine working in and through him. And this is both the challenge and the promise of Jesus. If we see him as 'God in a man-suit', we cannot possibly expect to be like him. But if we let go of the idea of God masquerading as a man, his every step predetermined from eternity, we discover the human Jesus who calls us to follow him, not by hoping to be godlike, but by being more fully what we are: human beings.

The real question we face with regard to Jesus is not, 'How is he different to the rest of us?' but 'How can we live in the liberating and joyous experience of God that he demonstrated?' Jesus did not become the person he was through a cosmic magic trick, but through his utter receptivity to God and to people. He was a man awake on the inside, when most around him were asleep.

As I have already said, I am a self-confessed Jesus freak. I love the Jesus I find in the Gospels, the man who championed the cause of the poor and the marginalised in his society, who treated women with dignity at a time when they were considered the chattels of a patriarchal society,

---

* Michael Dowd, *Earthspirit: A Handbook for Nurturing an Ecological Christianity* (Twenty-third Publications, 1991).

who spoke forgiveness to a dying thief while he himself was nailed to a wooden cross. Yet the Spirit of Jesus is not limited to that historic character in Palestine: I also love the Christ-figures in our world today. Also, I relish those moments when in the most unexpected circumstances, or through the most unlikely people, Christ bursts through a veneer of social inhumanity to show us afresh what being fully human can mean.

When my friend Mike recently attended a book launch at Kings College, London, he found himself chatting over a glass of wine with a woman who soon revealed her narrow religious outlook. As well as castigating homo-sexuals (Mike is gay, though she did not know this), she went on to describe Muslims as agents of Satan, who worship a false God.

Glad to be out of that conversation, Mike eventually left the college and made his way to the London Underground. As he walked down the escalator, he slipped and tumbled down several steps in what could have been a much worse accident. Slightly dazed, he was helped to his feet by a kind man in Muslim dress. He checked that Mike was all right, and then disappeared into the crowd. As Mike cautiously made his way forward, he reflected on the irony of this living parable, and quietly thanked God for a Christly figure in Muslim attire.

10. What Jesus really cared about

and it wasn't starting a new religion!

*Jesus came proclaiming the Kingdom of God,
and what arrived was the Church.*

Alfred F. Loisy

When the writer Louis Fischer visited Gandhi's ashram in 1942, he noticed a picture of Jesus hanging on the wall. It was the only picture or decoration in the room, and bore the caption, 'He is our peace.'

'But you are not a Christian,' Fischer told Gandhi.

'I am a Christian and a Hindu and a Muslim and a Jew,' Gandhi replied.

'Then you are a better Christian than most Christians,' Fischer thought to himself.

For more than forty years Gandhi spent two hours each day in meditation – an hour in the morning and an hour in the evening. Much of the time was spent in silence, but he always read from the Sermon on the Mount in the New Testament, and from the *Bhagavad Gita*, the Hindu scriptures. 'I have not been able to see any difference between the Sermon on the Mount and the *Bhagavad Gita*,' he once said.

For Gandhi, the Sermon on the Mount* was the core of Christ's teaching. He said it went straight to his heart, filling him with bliss, and quenching the agony of his soul. He also thought it held the keys for creating a better future for India and the world. In a conversation with Lord Irwin, the former British Viceroy of India, Gandhi was asked what he thought would solve the problems between Britain and India. He picked up a Bible and turned to the fifth chapter of Matthew and said, 'When your country and mine shall get together

---

* The Sermon on the Mount is a collection of sayings and teachings of Jesus, which is found in Matthew, chapters 5, 6 and 7.

on the teachings laid down by Christ in the Sermon on the Mount, we shall have solved the problems not only of our countries but those of the world.'

When I discovered that Gandhi read from the New Testament every day for forty years, I immediately went out and bought a copy of the *Bhagavad Gita*, of which I was completely ignorant. I felt that if he studied the Christian Bible, I would like to contemplate the Hindu scriptures. I also wanted to find out what it was in them that Gandhi thought resembled the teaching of Jesus.

My attention was soon drawn to a section that the translator entitled 'The Way of Love', where Sri Krishna, an incarnation of the Lord, instructs his friend and disciple Arjuna, who represents anyone who tries to live a spiritual life in the midst of everyday activities. This is what he says:

> *That one I love, who is incapable of ill will, who*
> *is friendly and compassionate. Living beyond*
> *the reach of 'I' and 'mine' and of pleasure and*
> *pain, patient, contented, self-controlled, firm*
> *in faith, with all their heart and all their mind*
> *given to me – with such people I am in love.*
> *Not agitating the world or by it agitated, they*
> *stand above the sway of elation, competition,*
> *and fear, accepting life: that one is beloved.*

They are detached, pure, efficient, impartial,
never anxious, selfless in all their undertakings;
they are my devotees, very dear to me.
That one is dear to me who runs not after the
pleasant or away from the painful, grieves not, lusts
not, but lets things come and go as they happen.

That devotee who looks upon friend and foe with
equal regard, who is not buoyed up by praise nor
cast down by blame, alike in heat and cold, pleasure
and pain, free from selfish attachments, the same
in honour as dishonour, quiet, ever full,
in harmony everywhere, firm in faith –
*such a one is dear to me.**

As a devoted Hindu, Gandhi loved the *Bhagavad Gita*, the best known of all Indian scriptures. It was his personal guidebook and constant inspiration in the struggle for India's independence. But much as he loved his own scriptures, he firmly believed that we should read the holy books of other traditions as well as our own, both to benefit from their wisdom, and also to discover the deep unity between the faiths.

---

* *The Bhagavad Gita*, translated by Eknath Easwaren (Nilgiri Press, 1985).

As a young man practising law in South Africa, Gandhi read the Bible avidly and at one point considered becoming a Christian. And so he decided to attend a church service. But as he climbed the steps of the large building and approached the entrance, his way was barred by a white church leader who asked, 'Where do you think you are going, kaffir?' Gandhi replied that he wanted to attend a church service. 'There's no room for kaffirs in this church,' the man snarled at him. 'Get out of here or I'll have my assistants throw you down the steps.'

From that point on, Gandhi decided to adopt what was good about Christianity, especially the teaching of Jesus, but he would never again consider becoming a Christian if it meant being part of the church. 'I like your Christ,' he famously remarked, 'I do not like your Christians. They are so unlike your Christ.'

In Gandhi's eyes, Jesus was a universal figure, 'the greatest source of spiritual strength that man has ever known', someone who could not belong solely to Christianity, but 'to all races and people, regardless of nationality, doctrine, faith or creed'.

In an article entitled 'What Jesus Means To Me', Gandhi wrote:

. . . he was certainly the highest example of one who wished to give everything, asking nothing in return, and not caring what creed might happen to be professed by the recipient. I am sure that if he were living here now among men, he would bless the lives of many who perhaps have never even heard his name, if only their lives embodied the virtues of which he was a living example on earth; the virtues of loving one's neighbour as oneself and of doing good and charitable works among one's fellowmen.*

Historically, Jesus was a Jew, from which he never wavered – a fact many Christians choose to ignore or consider inconsequential. Yet while remaining a devout Jew, he also transcended the religious oppositions of his day, most obviously in his positive attitude towards the Samaritans, who were hated and considered religious deviants by the Jews. He also praised the faith of a Roman centurion, another hated figure to his people, and a man who would probably have been a polytheist. Jesus also stood corrected by a pagan Canaanite woman who uncovered his discriminatory attitude towards her and her people.

None of these people were told to change their

---

* 'What Jesus Means To Me', in *The Modern Review*, October 1941.

religion; that wasn't his agenda. Jesus had no creed or dogma for his disciples to sign up to, no organisation to join. He simply called them to follow him, to be part of his way, which was a way of friendship, justice and inclusion.

As history unfolded, Jesus became the figurehead of the largest religion in the world. Yet I cannot believe that he ever intended to start a religion. Christianity appeared after his death in the first century, and not as a result of any directive from him. Yes, he commissioned his disciples to preach the good news and make disciples or followers of the way of life he embodied, but there is no indication that this would amount to starting a new religion.

That said, this does not mean that Jesus did not have a programme. Clearly, he intended to reconnect people to God and to the spiritual core of their tradition, but he also intended to restore a peasant community that was under acute strain from Roman colonisation by announcing a God of radical justice and a society of utter equality.

Jesus called this programme of spiritual and social renewal 'the kingdom of God'. It was his passion; throughout the Gospels he refers to it over one hundred and forty times. But its meaning is infamously tricky to pin down.

In many people's minds, the kingdom of God means where we go when we die (provided we believe the right things, that is). Matthew inadvertently reinforces this idea in his Gospel because of his preference for 'kingdom of heaven'.[*] Yet nothing could be further from what Jesus taught. 'The kingdom of God is among you,' he said. No one doubts that there is a future dimension to the kingdom, but it is absolutely and emphatically not about 'pie in the sky when you die'.

Personally, I think of the kingdom of God as a parallel reality, an alternative dimension alongside our sensory world, which we may awaken to, and which has the power to transform our lives, our communities and the world. The kingdom of God has come near, Jesus told his listeners.[†] The Gospel of Thomas (an early Christian text not included in the New Testament) expands on this, with Jesus saying that the kingdom of God is 'already spread out on the earth, but people aren't aware of it'.[‡] We don't die into the kingdom of God; we wake up to it. It is there all the time, waiting to be perceived and experienced.

But how does this happen? How do we become aware

---

[*] Matthew's Gospel is written for a Jewish audience, who did not use the word 'God' out of reverence for its holiness, so the writer uses the expression 'kingdom of heaven'.

[†] Matthew 10:7.

[‡] The Gospel of Thomas, saying 113.

of the kingdom of God? According to Jesus we discover it through repentance – a word that has now become a rather ugly piece of religious jargon, associated with feelings of guilt and shame. However, the Greek term *metanoia* from which the English word is translated actually has nothing to do with religion, much less guilt or shame. It literally means to go 'beyond the mind' or 'into the large mind'. It suggests a complete refocus of attention, a double take, a different way of thinking that expands our outlook – waking up to a new reality in which we see the world and ourselves in a different light.

Sometimes the awakening may be sudden and dramatic, as it was with George, a man I met years ago. I could write a whole volume just about my experiences with George. When we first met, he was a petty criminal who cheated on his wife and was renowned for his violence and anti-social behaviour. There was a back-story that accounted in part for the way he was, but he had progressed down a road that apparently anaesthetised him to the hurt he caused to himself and others.

One day, a concerned intermediary brought us together. I was a young church minister, wet behind the ears, but with relentless zeal. I spent hours with George, trying to convince him that there was another way to live, trying to lead him to repentance, but my words fell on deaf ears. Then, one night at about 3am in a drunken state, he telephoned and demanded that I go to his house; '. . . and bring your Christ with you!' he snorted down the phone.

Half an hour later, I stood on his doorstep, a naïve servant of God, faced with a threatening, out-of-control man, who menacingly removed my glasses as if preparing to throw one of his very large fists at me. 'Why would you want to hurt me, George?' I asked. My childlike openness and lack of fear somehow hit a switch in his conscious-ness. In an instant, he fell to his knees and broke into great sobs, begging me to pray for him.

That night, George awoke to a different reality, his sobs not simply for the threat he'd deliberately posed towards me, but for years of damage caused to himself and his loved ones which suddenly flashed before him. It was as if a great alarm clock suddenly rang out in his head, and he'd awoken from the nightmare and realised what he had become.

George's life was turned inside out; a new conscious-ness blossomed in which he was no longer an isolated predator up against the world, but someone who knew what it was to love and be loved. Of course, this was just the start of his journey. There were setbacks (and therein lies the further volume waiting to be penned). But his life would never be the same again. He repented, escaped the small mind of his ego-driven torment, entered the 'large mind' of God's love for him, and discovered an entirely new existence, a new reality.

For most of us, the process is more gradual. Perhaps a traumatic or joyful experience rouses the spirit, but instead of instantly bouncing out of our stupor, we toss and turn our way into consciousness, rubbing our eyes and slowly refocusing on the world. Eventually we wake up to new possibilities, once beyond our imagination. Conversion it certainly is, but it is more of a conversion process than an instant transformation.

It is also important to stress that this process may have nothing directly to do with religion, but may come about through counselling or therapy, through joining Alcoholics Anonymous, through the loss of a loved one or the birth of a child, or through a random everyday epiphany that modestly opens up a new sense of hope and possibility and takes us into the 'large mind'. It is the kingdom of God in action: the birth of a new consciousness that can change everything. It happens to Christians, Hindus, Muslims, Buddhists, agnostics, atheists . . . whoever. The kingdom of God knows no boundaries, acknowledges no religious borders.

Of course, to some people, the expression 'kingdom of

God' is problematic, perhaps because of its religious associations, or because it suggests a top-down hierarchy, or because it employs patriarchal language. However, this is not how Jesus spoke of it.

To begin with, surprisingly, both in Greek, the language of the Gospels, and in Aramaic, the home tongue of Jesus, 'kingdom' is a feminine, not masculine term. So, whereas in English it conveys the idea of royal power, dominion, privilege and hierarchy, the feminine word that Jesus used may indicate something more egalitarian, liberating and empowering. Certainly, this is how he spoke of the kingdom when he turned accepted values on their head, telling his followers, for example, that anyone who wished to be great in the kingdom of heaven must become the servant of all; or by announcing to the leaders of the synagogue that tax collectors and prostitutes were entering the kingdom of God ahead of them.

John Dominic Crossan, one of the world's leading Jesus scholars, very helpfully translates 'kingdom of God' as 'companionship of empowerment', a turn of phrase not unlike Martin Luther King's 'beloved community', a place where people are enabled to be who they are, and empowered to become what they might be.

This is precisely what we witness in the ragtag community that Jesus created, when he shared meals with people who were marginalised and disregarded by the religious establishment, and hung out with so called 'sinners'. He empowered women by treating them as equal human beings; he made room for misfits and dropouts, and he enabled a bunch of peasants, ultimately, to change the world.

The kingdom of God does not exist simply among religious people. Wherever the disadvantaged are empowered, wherever justice is practised, wherever the excluded are brought in, wherever friendship conquers prejudice and suspicion, wherever beauty is treasured and imagination liberated, or when truth is prized regardless of whoever speaks it – there is the kingdom of God.

In the course of my work as a parish priest, I find that the kingdom of God materialises in the most unlikely places. For example in a pub when a drunken woman beckons me to join her and her friends on the other side of the room, and I end up listening to stories of sorrow and hardship, then hold their hands and say a prayer with them.

Then there was Robert's funeral, which I took recently. I knew that he had no known next of kin, so I was surprised to find fourteen people at Robert's service, the staff of his care home. Sean, the manager of the home, gave a lovingly prepared eulogy, speaking with warmth and humour about a penniless North Londoner. I then left the lectern and sat among the congregation and asked them to tell me about Robert. They'd only known him for the last five years of his life, but stories rolled out, laughter was shared, and tears shed.

While he had no known family, Robert was not alone in life or death, but part of a beloved community, a true family of friends that gave him worth and identity. One lovely lady spoke of taking him home every year for Christmas dinner with her family – a lowly care home domestic, but a Jesus-figure to Robert! People spoke Robert's name with affection, friendship, and a twinkle in the eye. I have no idea whether anyone present was religious, but I drove home feeling that the kingdom of God had broken into the East Chapel at Golders Green that day.

In his refreshing rewrite of the New Testament, John Henson describes the kingdom of God as 'the Bright New World', a world that Jesus opened up and embodied. The Sermon on the Mount, which Gandhi loved so much, was Christ's manifesto for the kingdom of God. The famous beatitudes that open the passage are bullet points for living in the large mind. John Henson translates them as follows:

- *Splendid are those who take sides with the poor:*
  they are citizens of the Bright New World.
- *Splendid are those who grieve deeply over misfortunes:*
  the more deeply they grieve, the stronger they become.
- *Splendid are the gentle:*
  the world will be safe in their hands.
- *Splendid are those who have a passion for justice:*
  they will get things done.
- *Splendid are those who make allowances for others:*
  allowances will be made for them.
- *Splendid are those who seek the best for others and not themselves:*
  they will have God for company.
- *Splendid are those who help enemies to be friends:*
  they will be recognized as God's true children.
- *Splendid are those who have a rough time of it because they stand up for what is right:*
  *they too are citizens of the Bright New World.**

The noticeable thing about the Sermon on the Mount is that it is not a doctrinal statement, but a call to action.

---

* John Henson, *Good as New: A Radical Retelling of the Scriptures* (O Books, 2004).

The heart of the gospel Jesus taught is not a set of dogmas or a religious theory, but a way of life. The conflicting Jewish religious factions of the day often tried to drag him into their debates, but his concern was much more directed at the way that people lived out their beliefs.

Frederick Buechner, one of my favourite writers, summarises my vision of God's kingdom magnificently when he says that the kingdom of God in the sense of holiness, goodness and beauty is as close as breathing and is crying out to be born both within ourselves and within the world. It is what we hunger for above anything else even when we have no idea about its name or any realisation that it's what we are starving to death for.

The Kingdom of God is where our best dreams come from and our truest prayers. We glimpse it at those moments when we find ourselves being better than we are and wiser than we know. We catch sight of it when at some moment of crisis a strength seems to come to us that is greater than our own strength. The Kingdom of God is where we belong. It is home, and whether we realize it or not, I think we are all of us homesick for it.*

---

* Frederick Buechner, *The Clown in the Belfry* (Harper-SanFrancisco, 1992).

11. God of dirt and passion

the carnality of grace

> *Incarnation, if it means anything more than a*
> *'once upon a time' story, means grace is carnal;*
> *healing comes through the flesh.*

> Sam Keen

Our honeymoon destination was modest to say the least – a slightly seedy caravan site in North Wales. But it was a relief to get there and to be on our own at last.

To be honest, we were still smarting from the embarrassment of confessing to our whole church congregation a couple of weeks earlier that Pat would be pregnant when we made our wedding vows. This may not be a big deal today, but trust me, in the 'swinging sixties', being 'up the duff' was definitely still a big deal, especially in a conservative church like ours.

But we were away from all that now, and beside the sea for a week. Perhaps it was the sea air, or the sense of relief I now felt, or the tantalising forbiddenness of ladies and gents using the same shower block, but I became obsessed with the idea of jumping into the shower with my new bride. Pat firmly refused to join me in the gents' showers (of course she did), so I volunteered to slip into the ladies' block with her under the cover of darkness.

However the fun was short-lived when we heard voices, and it became clear that two women were waiting to use the shower after us. Stricken with guilt, we stood stock-still and silent, wondering what to do. At which point, the water ran out . . . we had no more change for the meter. Mortified, and covered in soap, we prepared for the walk of shame.

Then, astonishingly, my frantic prayer was answered: one of the women remembered she had left her shampoo in the caravan and disappeared to fetch it. Following which, the other woman decided to 'spend a penny'. Still covered in soap, we grabbed our chance, shot out of the shower and skulked into the night, back to the asylum of our tiny caravan.

Why, in heaven's name, I have asked myself many times since, could we not simply have walked out of the shower, grinned at the ladies, and laughed the whole thing off.

I come from a church background where sex was hardly mentioned, except in disapproving tones, or with shuffling discomfort. Certainly, we could never laugh about sex. Jokes about sex were 'dirty', 'vulgar' and definitely ungodly. If sex were ever talked about in a positive way it would be with solemnity. Oddly enough, in the same way that we spoke about God! Indeed, come to think of it, these were the two things we were never allowed to make fun of: sex, and God.

The first Christian writer I came across who appeared to subvert this typical po-faced religious attitude towards sex was C.S. Lewis. In his book *The Four Loves*, he says he can hardly help regarding it as one of God's jokes that a passion so soaring as Eros should be linked in 'incongruous symbiosis' with a bodily appetite like sex. We need to be continually reminded, says Lewis, that we are composite creatures, rational animals, akin on the one hand to the angels, on the other to tomcats. 'It is a bad thing not to be able to take a joke', he writes. 'Worse, not to take a divine joke; made, I grant you, at our expense, but also (who doubts it?) for our endless benefit.'*

And yes, it is true: there is a delightful absurdity about two bodies writhing around in sweaty fervour: feeling, groping, stroking and caressing with ever-increasing urgency until finally collapsing in a gratified heap, laughing or at least grinning from ear to ear.

No wonder jokes about sex abound in every language and culture in the world. Some are funny. Many are dull or disgusting. All of them are old. Yet as Lewis observes, they represent an attitude to sex that endangers the Christian life far less than reverential gravity. Sadly, the point is lost on many churchgoers who still adhere to what Lewis calls the 'ludicrous and portentous solemnisation of sex'. If sex really is a divine joke these people definitely don't get it. Furthermore, they fully intend to wipe the grin off the face of anyone who does.

Even now, I cringe when I look back on two naïve youngsters (I was just nineteen when we jumped into the shower), madly in love and innocent as the day is long, suffering such mental torment simply because our enthusiastic passion for each other overflowed in the

---

* C.S. Lewis, *The Four Loves* (Collins, 1960).

'premature' arrival of our first child. For years, we avoided telling anyone that our lovely Jeni was conceived out of wedlock – until she outed us at an anniversary party!

The real shame lies with those who prudishly load young people with guilt simply for being normal, but who cannot bring themselves to have a decent conversation with them about what it means to be magnificent, passionate, embodied human beings.

It seems ironic to me that Christians should have such a struggle with carnality and sensual delight when we claim to worship the one who created physical bodies – and presumably therefore also invented hanky-panky. More importantly, Christianity is founded on the idea that the divine became enfleshed in a human body, complete with all the usual 'bits' and experiencing all the desires and urges that go with that.

Yet, even today, in the twenty-first century, the church still can't find the carnality in grace. Most of the sticky issues that trouble the faithful revolve around some aspect of sexuality: celibacy, contraception, divorce and remarriage, homosexuality, or cohabitation. God knows how many people have suffered, or been alienated from Christianity, by the church's attitude towards these subjects.

So where does all this distrust of bodiliness originate? Some of it certainly traces back to the Bible where menstruating women, and men who have ejaculated, are treated as unclean, and where a battle seems to be set up between the 'flesh' and the Spirit.

That said, the Bible also contains many positive references to sexual passions and relations. There are passages which if translated into the vernacular could turn many a face in the pews bright red. The story of Ruth and Boaz on the threshing floor is a pretty good example. Then there is the Song of Songs, a collection of erotic poems that throbs between the covers of the Bible, gloriously celebrating human sexual desire and bodiliness for its own sake. Preachers and commentators through the centuries have hideously turned the book into an allegory of God's love for Israel, or Christ's love for the church, while the real meaning is delightfully obvious. If John Milton is correct in assuming that simplicity and sensuousness are the basic ingredients of poetry in any language, then the Song of Songs needs no convoluted interpretation. It is what it is: a repertoire of highly sophisticated eroticism.*

I love the fact that a book which has been described as the most sensuous book in all the writings of antiquity

---

* Comments on The Song of Songs are inspired by Marcia Falk, *The Song of Songs* (HarperCollins, 1990), and essays from Harold Bloom (ed.), *The Song of Songs* (Chelsea House Publishers, 1988).

and which makes no direct reference to God is included in Holy Scripture. Perhaps it made its way into the Bible because of its popular appeal – around 100 CE, Rabbi Akiba felt obliged to warn anyone singing the Song of Songs in wine taverns, treating it as a vulgar song, that they would forfeit their share in the world to come.

The ancient Jews appeared to have less hang-ups about sex than many modern-day Christians. They believed that natural forces are a good creation of God; that the divine could be sensed through pleasant experiences like sexual love. The Jewish wedding ceremony concludes: 'Blessed be thou, O Lord . . . who hast created joy and gladness, groom and bride, jubilation and exultation, pleasure and delight, love, brotherliness, peace and friend-liness . . . Blessed be thou, O Lord, who makest the groom rejoice with his bride.' One ancient rabbi actually argued that we would someday give account to God for all the good things which our eyes beheld but which we refused to enjoy.

If sensuousness in relationships is encouraged in the Song of Songs and in the Jewish community that inter-preted it, why is it that for most of Judaeo-Christian history this outlook has been muted, if not silenced alto-gether? Why have we ended up with a disapproving God, whose chief sexual ethic seems to be abstinence, or at least, 'do it but don't enjoy it'? I tend to agree with Dora Russell, wife of the famous agnostic philosopher Bertrand Russell, when she said, 'There is no instinct that has been so maligned, suppressed, abused, and distorted by religious teaching as the instinct of sex.'

Recently, I counselled a man in his mid-fifties who suffered from near psychotic levels of guilt, much of which traced back to his teenage experience of battling unsuccessfully with masturbation. His impression was that no proper Christian would do such a thing; that God severely disapproved of it. And so he fought against his emotional urges for all he was worth. 'But I never managed it,' he said. 'I never did stop masturbating. I passed into my twenties feeling like a massive failure – and a fraud every time I went forward for communion or even stepped into a church. So I gave up fighting it. But the guilt never went away.' At times he felt so bad about his body, which constantly 'led him into sin', that he just wanted to escape from it, and considered committing suicide.

This man's problem was fairly extreme, yet his fundamental dilemma is all too common in some Christian circles. His sense of wanting to escape from the body with its temptations is rooted in a widespread theology of alienation – the idea that we do not really belong in this physical world, that we are exiled here until God transports us to our heavenly home far away. While we are here, we must battle with the lusts of the flesh, and try to get the upper hand over them. The upshot is a neurotic spirituality that leaves people at war with their own embodied humanity.

Historically, Christianity has never escaped some of the worst elements of Gnosticism, which infected the early church. This involved a radical opposition between the material and spiritual worlds, between the physical body and the soul. This influence permeated the ancient world at the beginning of the Christian era. And while in theory the church rejected any kind of dualism between body and spirit, in practice dualism has massively shaped and influenced the spirituality of western Christianity, in particular.

Throughout the history of the church, from Clement of Alexandria and Origen through Augustine and down to the present day, a dualism between the material and the spiritual, between body and spirit, has characterised much, maybe most, of Christianity. The outcome has been a basic mistrust of the body and bodily desires, and a sense of dislocation from the physical world, which becomes a place simply to journey through, rather than call home.

What many who have turned their back on dualistic Christianity long for is a spirituality of belonging, a sense of feeling at home in this world, of belonging in the body with its passions and appetites and its deep harmony with nature and the earth. Instead of seeing the spiritual journey as a passage out of physical and material reality in order to encounter God in some 'higher' dimension, we look to discover the divine within this world of bodies and dirt and passion. So yes, as my friend Martin Wroe puts it in one of his poems, there is 'a sacrament of getting laid'.

Of course, this is not to say that every experience of getting laid is sacramental, that every passion should be gratified. Sometimes, indulging our appetites can prove a profoundly alienating experience, utterly devoid of grace.

Sitting in the pub one day, a young man asked if he could buy me a drink (it's a perk of wearing a clerical collar). 'Do you stretch to a single malt?' I asked with a grin. A few minutes later, with small talk out of the way and a double whisky in my hand, he told me that he feared he was a sex addict. 'I just can't stop myself,' he said. 'I've slept with six women so far this month, and we're only halfway through it . . . The trouble is, I'm feeling emptier and emptier on the inside. And I'm finding it harder and harder to look the women in the eye afterwards.' Apparently, he had attempted several times to take a break from sex – including during Lent, despite not being a religious person – but all his efforts came to nothing. And he felt even emptier.

Sam Keen, a popular writer on spirituality, describes the dilemma of realising that neither religion, nor secular culture, gave him a satisfactory framework to understand his identity as a physical being. He writes:

> *What has happened to me? How am I to understand this warmth and grace which pervades my body? As I begin to reflect, I realise that neither the Christian nor the secular culture, in which I have been jointly nurtured, have given me adequate categories to interpret such an experience. Neither has taught me to discern the sacred in the voice of the body and the language of the senses. In the same measure that Christian theology has failed to help me appreciate the* carnality of grace, *secular ideology has failed to provide me categories for understanding* the grace of carnality. *Before I can understand what I have experienced, I must see where Christian theology and secular ideology have failed me.***

The 'carnality of grace' amounts to a realisation that we never encounter God outside of our fleshly experience.

---

* Sam Keen, *To a Dancing God* (HarperCollins, 1970).

All grace is embodied. We discover the divine in sunshine and rain, in cream cakes and green vegetables, in bread and wine and water, in lovemaking and digging the garden, in a hot bath and dirt beneath the nails. We are embodied beings living entirely within a physical world. And while God is far greater than the sum of physical things, divinity resides in dirt and delight, passion and tears, green grass and furry creatures. If we cannot discover the carnality of grace, we cannot discover grace at all.

The 'grace of carnality' is the recognition that the world is infused with divine Spirit, and that our sense of meaning and purpose as human beings rests in the discovery of that Spirit. The grace of carnality is the realisation that the universe is a sacrament – a means of connecting us with the very Ground of our Being, which we sometimes call 'God'. You do not need to be narrowly religious, or believe in God, in order to experience a deep-down satisfaction in the world, but you do need to have the sense that life is about more than your own ego-driven passions and desires. It's about love and relationship, gratitude and humility, awe and wonder and curiosity. It's about much more than just skating across the surface of physical existence; it's about touching the depth of things, feeling the heights.

The man in the pub wasn't a sex addict; just a hungry soul who hadn't yet discovered the larder. 'What are you looking for?' I asked him. 'What is it that you miss when you try to give up sleeping with someone?' He paused for thirty seconds, which seemed like an eternity, then, frighteningly, he replied, 'I'm trying to find my mother.' It turned out that when he was seven his mother had twins. And after that he never remembers his mother cuddling him or saying that she loved him. Now, she was long dead and had become an idealised figure in his psyche with whom no woman on earth could ever compare.

There was no simple answer for him – not even another single malt could buy him that. But he began to see that the answer did not lie in interminable surfing of sexual passions and faceless partners. Hard work lay ahead for him, perhaps with a therapist who could help him to face his loss and move on: to find some grace in his carnality – a relationship of faithful intimacy and true otherness.

In the end all carnality can lead to grace if we look deeply enough into it and pursue its truest longing. We may not experience the painful craving that my whisky-supplying friend felt, but we all yearn for more than purely physical gratification.

In a lecture entitled 'The Secret Life of the Love Song', the rock singer Nick Cave argues that, ultimately, all love songs address God for it is the haunted areas of longing that the true love song inhabits. The love song, he says, is a howl in the void for love and comfort, which begins on the lips of a child crying for its mother. The love song is the sound of our endeavours to become godlike, to rise above the earthbound and the mediocre.

Sometimes those who are weary with the Bible, or just unattracted to it, ask me if God wrote anything else. Gladly, I tell them, yes, God's other book is the book of nature, written in trees and ice and frogs and dung beetles, but also in our bodies and in our hearts. This other book of God is a dirty book, an earthy, carnal tome soaked in sweat and blood and tears, oozing dark passion and sensuous delight.

We read the other book of God as sacramental – the divine mediated in earthly form. Unlike dogmas and creeds, sacraments are sensed, and the physical world of bodies, passions and nature is a sensual book, as well as a dirty book. But it is the Other Book of God: holy and sacred as any other scripture.

Frankly, I am fed up with 'other-worldly' Christian spirituality, with the piety that leaves people feeling alienated from their own selves, their bodies, and from the physical world of nature. I have had enough of the guilt-inducing religion that makes a misery of lives and fails monumentally to celebrate the gift of life. I want to stand on God's good earth and know I belong. I believe in a God who inhabits bodies, who is comfortable with human passion, who dances to the rhythms of nature and feels the beat of a lover's heart, who feasts on friendship and drinks to the health of our planet, who sees the plight of the poor and needy and never says, 'There, there. You will be all right when you get to heaven.'

12. Cigars, chocolate and other holy sacraments

a world crammed with heaven

I would like a great lake of beer for the King of kings, I would like to be watching heaven's family drinking it through all eternity.

Attributed to Brigid

I cannot recall when I first met Tony Littler, but I will never forget my last encounter with him – in one of the most powerful and moving ceremonies I have yet had the privilege to conduct.

For ten years prior to his death, Tony suffered from Pick's disease, a form of dementia. At his funeral, he was described as a larger than life, loveable, infuriating lion of a man whose presence could fill the room. He certainly wasn't a man you could easily ignore.

One of my strongest memories of Tony is talking with him after the meeting in the House of Lords where his daughter, my dear friend Aimie, launched a campaign against sex trafficking. I especially remember his pride at what she was doing.

Tony was a colourful man, full of paradoxes, extremes and endearing idiosyncrasies. He was a scientist with razor-sharp logic, who was also obsessed with the sentiment and romance of the film *Mama Mia*. He loved smoking fine cigars, tucking into a pork pie with piccalilli, lighting fires in the garden, and lying in the grass gazing into heaven. He was even once arrested for stealing a policeman's hat!

The world is certainly a greyer place without Tony.

The plan was for him to travel to London for his other daughter Jenna's wedding, but as the time approached, it became clear that he would not be up to the journey. So we planned a small prenuptial ceremony for Jenna and Philipp in the church opposite Tony's care home.

In the dying embers of a late autumn day, we sat in a semi-circle in the chancel area of the church, the fading

174

light pierced only by a couple of dozen small candles in jam jars. There, in that magical, warm glow, I led Jenna and Philipp through a simple Celtic ceremony of betrothal in which they exchanged stones which each had chosen from the seafront that morning, and I blessed their future marriage.

After this, Tony's wife Hanna and his daughters each took turns to sit at his side, hold his hand, and thank him for some specific gift he had brought to their life. There were stories of humour, wisdom and love – and not a few tears.

How much Tony understood of what was going on, we will never know. But he rallied and seemed to pay attention, looking at each of them as they spoke. One by one, everyone kissed him, after which I anointed his head and blessed him in Christ's name. We then brought Art – Aimie and Rob's little boy, Tony's grandson – into the circle, and I blessed him too. It was one of the holiest moments of my priestly life, filled with an awesome sense of what lay ahead for these three generations of people.

Afterwards in the care home, a bottle of Champagne was popped, and we toasted Jenna and Philipp – and Tony too. Aimie helped her dad to a glass. Someone asked if he should be drinking Champagne. She said he could have whatever he wanted! Everyone agreed.

Just a couple of weeks later, I conducted Tony's funeral.

But that is not the end of the story. Jenna and Philipp went on to have a magnificent wedding in London just before Christmas, where Tony's name was mentioned. And we raised a glass to him and had the joyful celebration Tony would have wished us to have. I even thought I glimpsed him loitering in the background, puffing on one of his cigars with a proud grin.

And speaking of Tony's cigars, I am delighted to report that Aimie gave me some of Tony's treasured collection as a thank you (it is known for me to enjoy the odd cigar or two). Some months later, on a country walk with Aimie, I pulled out one of the cigars and offered her a puff. She gladly accepted. And in some wonderful way, as she did this, she felt the distinct sense of her daddy's presence with us on the walk – mediated by a sacred puff of smoke.

Aimie isn't a smoker, but since Tony's death she says she uses his cigars to reach for communion with him. 'I light them on his birthday, and death day,' she told me. 'And recently, as a family we jointly smoked one while sitting on a beautiful oak bench that we had commissioned for his favourite spot overlooking the Dorset vales and coastline. It is a sacred act of communion for me and those I share it with: remembering, saying thank you, and smiling.'

It is very strange how something totally commonplace like puffing on a cigar can immediately take you to another place, or bring someone back to life in your consciousness, or reproduce a feeling from a bygone era. It is not a conjuring trick. There is nothing magic about a cigar (except what is always magic about a good cigar), yet, amazingly, it can become a medium to communicate the presence of a place or person or event.

Sometimes when I pour a jug of water into the font before christening a baby, I will remind the congregation that it is just a jug of water from the church tap – a pint or two of Holloway's best. It contains no supernatural qualities, despite my prayer of blessing, yet we pour it forth in the hope and expectation that it will be a means of communicating God's love and ours to the child.

It is like when we buy a box of chocolates for a loved one: we do so in the hope that it will become much more than a box of chocolates, that it will somehow bear our love and affection to the other person. Sitting on the shelf in the shop before we bought it, it was nothing more than a cardboard container with twenty or thirty chocolates. But once purchased, lovingly wrapped, labelled and passed on to the beloved with an intimate kiss, it takes on a new reality; it becomes so much more than a box of chocolates.

I still have a couple of packets of Tony's cigars. Each time I light one Tony comes to life in my mind. This is the power of symbol, or sacrament as we call it in the church: whether a cigar, a chocolate or a jug of water, it conveys something way beyond its intrinsic value or quality.

I once took the funeral of a man who was a huge fan of John Wayne, star of over eighty westerns. A pair of size-fourteen cowboy boots stood on top of the coffin throughout the service. When I visited the man's widow beforehand to plan the funeral, the boots were on a table beside the fire, along with various other items of John Wayne memorabilia, plus some pictures of her beloved husband: a shrine to 'Duke' and one of his greatest fans. Just before the curtains closed at the crematorium, I removed the boots and handed them to the grief-stricken widow, who hugged them to her breast, sobbing inconsolably. It was as if she actually held her husband. No one in that place imagined that this was *merely* a pair of boots.

Why is it that we limit the notion of sacraments to a religious context, administered by priests in solemn ceremonies, when the world is literally crammed with them? Every single day people – who may not consider themselves in the least religious – participate in, and administer, holy sacraments in all kinds of ways.

Sacrament

by Martin Wroe

The Sacrament of a joke, the funniest story
The Sacrament of tears in your eyes

The Sacrament of a meal, slowly cooking,
The Sacrament of a round glass of wine

The Sacrament of a child's first, wide-eyed, steps
The Sacrament of all that trust in you

The Sacrament of bass, drum, guitar
The Sacrament connected to the . . . hip bone

The Sacrament of being there, right place, right time
The Sacrament of a listening ear

The Sacrament of the novel you can't put down
The Sacrament of the poem with no rhyme

The Sacrament of starlings, in V-formation
The Sacrament of eye-contact (with a dog)

The Sacrament of a lie-in, the long-weekend
The Sacrament of getting paid or getting laid

The Sacrament of your sweet lips on mine
The Sacrament of You and Me

The Sacrament of friendship, rough and smooth
The Sacrament of the days, the months, the years

The Sacrament of questions with no answers
The Sacrament of silence. Enough said

The Sacrament of a life baptised by love
The Sacrament of the divine
In bread and wine.

It is absolutely not the case that some things are intrinsically holy while others are inherently profane, or that some people are blessed with God's presence while others are not. God lurks in every atom of the universe, every creature on earth, every moment in time, every human experience. Nothing need be done in order to invoke the presence of divinity; God surrounds us like fresh air. All that is necessary is to wake up to that presence, to become aware of it. In her book *Waiting for God*, the French philosopher Simone Weil makes the point that attention is the chief means by which our souls encounter God. Spirituality is just that: the art of paying attention.

Elizabeth Browning expresses a similar thought in her poem 'Aurora Leigh', where she makes reference to the biblical story of Moses looking after his father-in-law's sheep in the desert when he sees a burning bush. In the passage from Exodus 3, Moses becomes curious because the fiery bush keeps burning and is not consumed. Then, as he approaches to see what is happening, a voice speaks out of the bush telling him to remove his shoes because the ground he is standing on is holy ground.

In her poem, Elizabeth Browning inspiringly tells us that, not just that particular patch of ground, but all ground is holy:

> *Earth's crammed with heaven,*
> *and every common bush afire with God;*
> *but only he who sees, takes off his shoes,*
> *the rest sit round it and pluck blackberries.*

Nothing is small or insignificant in the world, Browning says. Even a humble chaffinch implies the cherubim. Even the little tremor of blood in her thin veined wrist utters distinctly the 'strong clamour of a vehement soul'. We can't tear apart the spiritual and the natural without losing sight of who or what God is about, she seems to be saying. God is in everything. God speaks from everything. It is just that, mostly, we don't see or hear this. We indeed sit round simply 'plucking blackberries' (or puffing smoke, or sucking a chocolate, or splashing water on a baby).

When Simone Weil makes the point that the chief means by which our souls encounter God is by paying attention, she is not saying that we must pay attention to God – not directly, anyway. Because, let's face it, we have no idea how to pay attention to God. God does not have a face, or a voice, or a physical presence, apart from the faces, voices and physical presences that are all around us.

In the story, God spoke to Moses out of the bush. But was there an actual audible voice? Could I have heard it if I had been there? Could it have been recorded? No, of course not. But that does not mean that it was not real. Moses heard God speak to him *through the act of paying attention*.

What causes all such things – a burning bush in the desert, a burning cigar in the Dorset countryside, a box of chocolates from a loved one, or bread and wine in the

Eucharist – to become sacraments, purveyors of a greater presence, human or divine, is the act of paying attention.

Jesus called people to *consider* the flowers of the field, the song of a bird. He told stories about grains of wheat, changes in the weather, a wedding feast, a woman baking bread, a man walking in a field who found a treasure, a lost sheep etc. Everything and anything was for Jesus a means of pointing people to God, who is the deeper reality within ordinary objects, activities and events.

Buddhism too lays great stress on paying attention to mundane things through the practice of 'mindfulness' – the art of being fully present in the moment. When the Buddha was asked, 'Sir, what do you and your monks practise?' he replied, 'We sit, we walk, and we eat.' The questioner continued, 'But sir, everyone sits, walks, and eats,' and the Buddha told him, 'When we walk, we *know* we are walking. When we eat, we *know* we are eating.' While Buddhists do not believe in God, as such, it strikes me that Buddhism is deeply sacramental; it senses the 'beyond' within the present; it tells us that grace and peace and compassion are transmitted through ordinary things, ordinary experiences.

And this 'beyond' in all things is what I call 'God'.

The central act in the rite of the Eucharist is remembering. Jesus said, 'Do this to remember me.' Remembering is, quite simply, an act of mindfulness, of paying attention to something that we might otherwise forget or lose. To remember is to *re-member*, to bring together or reassemble.

Much of life is spent in forgetfulness. We eat and drink, and interact with those we love in a kind of sleepwalking semi-existence. We take for granted the things we rely on – the air we breathe, the food on our plate, the transport system that gets us to work, the people who collect our rubbish, the sound of the birds in the trees, the TV we relax in front of. Somehow the very momentum of daily activity lulls us into a state of forgetfulness, an unconscious stupor – until the people or things are not there, and we wake up to an absence.

The Vietnamese Zen master and poet, Thich Nhat Hanh, who has written about the synchronicities between Buddhism and Christianity, sees the practice of the Eucharist as a practice of awareness. He writes: 'When Jesus broke the bread and shared it with his disciples, he said, "Eat this. This is my flesh." He knew that if his disciples would eat one piece of bread in mindfulness, they would have real life.'

For me, participation in the Eucharist is a wake-up call, a regular reminder that I easily fall asleep on the inside. It may seem strange, but a pinch of bread and a sip of wine in the company of friends and fellow travellers reconnect me with all that I love and admire about the figure of Jesus and rekindle my commitment to follow his way. The Eucharist also reawakens in me the realisation that the world itself is a divine sacrament; that there is no rift between the sacred and the profane, the religious and the non-religious, the spiritual and the physical.

Sacraments are ordinary things, ordinary events and experiences that help us to re-member, to reassemble that which feels absent or torn apart. In the Christian narrative, the sacraments of bread and wine reconnect us with the Spirit of Christ, but sacraments in the greater sense can reconnect us with loved ones we feel we have lost, with loved ones who are still with us but who we easily forget, with what it means to be living, breathing creatures of God's earth.

13. You are the dark of the world

not a God for goodie-goodies

Accepting the reality of our broken, flawed lives is the beginning of spirituality not because the spiritual life will remove our flaws but because we let go of seeking perfection and, instead, seek God, the one who is present in the tangledness of our lives.

Michael Yaconelli

'So you are the villains' priest, eh?' a big burly man asked when I arrived at Golders Green crematorium for the funeral of Ronnie Biggs, the Great Train Robber.

His friend chipped in: 'That's what you should call your autobiography, father: *The Villains' Priest?* I'd buy that.'

I grinned, taking the ascription as a compliment. Meanwhile, traffic outside the crematorium was at a standstill. Banks of photographers with stepladders and long lenses lined the pavement. Even when he is dead, Ronnie Biggs is still massive news.

It wasn't my first Great Train Robber's funeral; I co-conducted Bruce Reynolds's service (the man credited with masterminding the robbery) almost a year earlier. On one level, the funerals of Biggs and Reynolds are no different from anyone else's. Yet it's hard to overlook who these men were: the perpetrators of one of the most audacious crimes of the century. And despite it being over fifty years since it took place, the culprits still attract great attention and arouse heated reactions.

After taking each of the funerals I received emails and messages criticising me for getting involved. I was accused of 'glorifying criminals', of presiding over immoral celebrations of unrepentant men, of shaming the church, God, and myself. Apart from anything else, this is an entirely mistaken line of argument. Conducting a person's funeral in no way implies approval of that person's life. If it did, I should take far fewer funerals. I may even struggle to find someone to take mine!

But what really troubles me about these sorts of reactions is the arrogant judgementalism. Some people appear not to notice that Jesus didn't hang out with the religious goodie-goodies; he mostly gave them a hard time. His extensive litany of 'woes' in Matthew 23, for example, is entirely directed at the scribes and Pharisees, the religious hoity-toity, who he describes as whitewashed tombs, which look beautiful on the outside, but inside are full of the bones of the dead and all kinds of filth.

By contrast, Jesus seemed comfortable spending time with sinners. So much so, he was accused of being their friend, of eating and drinking with them, and of being a glutton and a drunkard himself. He attended a feast at the house of a publican and invited himself to the house of Zacchaeus, the tax collector, where he was accused of being a guest of a sinner. This rankled Jesus so much, he told the temple authorities that the tax collectors and prostitutes would enter the kingdom of heaven ahead of them.

But were these sinners repentant sinners? Was that why he was comfortable with them? That isn't made clear. If they were, it was the presence of Jesus that brought them to repentance. The sort of attitude that says, 'You're welcome here provided you come on our terms' is the antithesis to everything Jesus stood for.

I constantly hear people refer to Ronnie Biggs as unrepentant. But how are we to know? Isn't that God's call? In his autobiography Biggs strongly denies the accusation that he had no regrets: 'I have always regretted the hurt I caused by my actions.' He also makes it clear that he (and he believes everyone involved in the robbery) absolutely regrets that Jack Mills (the train driver) was injured during the robbery and was put under such pressure during and after the trial. He apologises to Mr Mills and his family and to everyone else affected in any way by what happened on 8 August 1963. He speaks of wishing he could turn the clock back, and says it is time to take responsibility for his life.

Does this constitute repentance? It's not for me to say. But I dislike the niggardly attitude that concentrates on the specks in other people's eyes while ignoring the planks in our own. Jesus himself said, 'Do not judge, so that you may not be judged' (Matthew 7:1). Yet there are those who appear to imagine that being moralistic and judgemental is a way of being faithful to Christ.

After Ronnie's funeral, many of us piled into a pub around the corner, where I had a stream of conversations with people who many would classify as 'sinners'. Yet what I discovered was a lot of goodness, a lot of love, and an awful lot of openness towards this particular 'man of the cloth' talking about Jesus. They are the sort of people I describe as 'bad Christians', the hordes of people who know their lives are a bit screwed up, who make no claim to be squeaky clean Christians, but whose hearts are open to God in all sorts of ways.

It's a sad fact that many people will never appear in church because they feel judged by those of us who call ourselves Christians. Meanwhile, Christ's arms remain open to all.

Probably the highlight of Ronnie's funeral for me was the tribute from his thirteen-year-old granddaughter Ingrid who spoke boldly and articulately about him. 'People have told me that my granddad was a train robber,' she said, 'but to me, he was my granddad, who played with me and made me laugh.' In a packed crematorium, with the world looking on, Ingrid came closer to reflecting God's view of Ronnie Biggs than anyone else; she saw him as a human being, not a celebrity criminal or the scoundrel he is often painted to be. She defined him by how she experienced him, not by events that took place decades before.

After the funeral, Michael and Veronica Biggs said that their youngest daughter Lily, Ingrid's sister, hadn't been christened, and asked if I would conduct the service at St Luke's. I felt honoured, and the thought of being involved in a more positive event with the family delighted me. So one week after Ronnie's funeral I did indeed baptise three-year-old Lily Biggs. It was a more intimate affair, with no paparazzi outside the church: a couple of dozen people gathered around the font, including one of the Hell's Angels who had led the cortège to the crematorium a week earlier. 'I've heard you got threats after taking Ronnie's funeral,' Ian said to me.

'Well, not exactly threats . . .' I replied.

'The boys weren't happy about that,' the burly biker said. 'If you have any more trouble, Dave, you just let me know.'

'I'll bear that in mind,' I responded, gratefully.

A simplistic interpretation of Christ's parable about the sheep and the goats envisages judgement day as a straightforward separation of 'goodies' from 'baddies'. But the reality is that there is a sheep *and a goat* in each one of us – there certainly is in me. Divine judgement has to be more sophisticated than simply telling the Ronnie Biggs of this world to stand on one side, and churchgoing Christians to stand on the other.

I love the work of Robert Lentz, the Franciscan icon painter, whose icons include images of unconventional saints like Albert Einstein, Black Elk, Steve Biko and Harvey Milk. When Lentz was commissioned to paint an icon of Jesus as the Good Shepherd, he agreed, with the proviso that there would be no cute woolly lambs anywhere near him. The Good Shepherd is about sinners, the people we push to the margins, Robert Lentz says, 'the ones we want to forget or even destroy. He is about addicts and sex-offenders and shysters and punks. If I am going to paint the Good Shepherd, he is going to be holding a goat, and not just any goat, a smelly, lustful, scary old billy goat.'[*]

As Robert Lentz points out, most medieval symbolism for the devil is derived from goat physiognomy. Having looked after the monastery goats, which he hated, Lentz says that you can smell them from quite a distance, and the expression 'horny' was originally applied to them. But his Christ would hug such a beast to remind puritanical Christians that God's ways are not to be confused with ours.

The Franciscan monk painted the goat, hair by hair, and was surprised at the end when it seemed ready to jump into his arms. 'There was too much of me in the goat that I did not want to acknowledge and see,' Lentz

---

[*] Robert Lentz and Edwina Gateley, *Christ in the Margins* (Orbis Books, 2009).

writes. 'He demanded that I embrace myself with compassion and look at other human beings with new understanding.'

Each of our souls has billy-goat parts – wild, untamed and undomesticated parts – that don't fit with our idealised image of ourselves or with how we wish to be seen, so we keep them hidden from public view.

I only met Ronnie Biggs once, at Bruce Reynolds's funeral, where I read out his tribute to his old pal and fellow train robber. Outside the church he greeted the mass of paparazzi cameras with two fingers raised. Ronnie Biggs, the celebrity train robber, was just that: a celebrity, a media figure who treated the press with the contempt with which he felt they treated him. But the Ronnie Biggs I met was a warm, charming and personable man. And I have good reason to believe that, far from being 'unrepentant', he had a heart that was wide open to God.

The point is that some people have the billy-goat side of their character paraded in the public eye, while most of us manage to keep it concealed. Yet Jesus never judged a person by their public persona; he looked with respect and compassion on those who were judged publicly to be 'sinners'; he looked to the heart of people and not just to their external appearance.

The question we all must face is not just whether we can love other people, but whether we can learn to love ourselves. The one follows the other. Can we love, not just the goodie-goodie bits of us, the parts we are proud of or which we can at least learn to live with, but also find compassion for the parts we conceal or refuse to confront, the wild, untamed parts?

In a similar way that Jungian psychology teaches us to acknowledge and integrate the shadow side of the personality, which is the seat of creativity, Robert Lentz believes that our billy-goat parts are potential treasure troves of spiritual energy that can be tamed and brought in from the margins. Puritanical people fear contamination from this energy, he says, and so cut themselves off and starve. 'Christ the Good Shepherd coaxes us back to wholeness and health.'

For many of us, the image of a billy goat replacing a lamb is disturbing. It is an affront to our dignity and serenity. But then the publicans and prostitutes that Jesus hung out with did not fit either; just as criminals and drug addicts don't fit today. They threaten our comfortable religion. But the Christ with the billy goat embraces them too.

The people I personally love and admire most are not the goody two-shoes types, but those who know their dark side and are able to channel its energy with good purpose: people like my friend Harry, an alcoholic who has been in recovery for twenty-five years.

Learning to live with something like alcoholism, and discovering how to channel the energy that often drives it in more positive directions, is no mean feat and requires a lifetime of practice. However, it is not just those who know the chaotic side of their personality that Robert Lentz's icon addresses but also the rest of us who know deep down that we too have a billy goat within – a wild, less domesticated side to our character, which we mostly keep out of sight. The Good Shepherd embraces the goat within each one of us, even when we struggle to embrace it ourselves.

Interestingly, the Twelve Step programme adopted by groups like Alcoholics Anonymous is finding increasingly wider appeal as a spiritual resource. The programme begins with a clear acknowledgement of the dark side to the personality and its potential to sink us into chaos, but it also recognises that there is a power greater than ours to draw on. Step three involves making a decision to turn one's will and life over to the care of this Higher Power, to God by whatever name.

Another great resource within Alcoholics Anonymous is the Serenity Prayer, which I constantly commend to people, not only as a succinct and powerful prayer, but also as a spiritual practice, a way of life.

> God grant me the serenity
> to accept the things I cannot change;
> courage to change the things I can;
> and wisdom to know the difference.

The important thing is not to try to contort myself into something I am not, but to redirect my energies in more positive directions. For example, the lustful energy that abuses people can also become a force to fight for social justice; the gluttony that hungers selfishly for new experiences can imaginatively seek to bring new joy into the lives of others.

Yet every alcoholic or addict – even someone like Harry who has been in recovery for a quarter of a century – knows that we are all still dancing in the dark, that even the best of us is just one bad choice away from screwing up and sinking into chaos. So we need humility. There can be no room for self-righteousness or judgement of others.

I once heard the wonderful Franciscan, Brother Ramon, ask why it is that religion makes some people so judgemental, so miserable, so legalistic, so fanatical, so bigoted, so violent? Why is it that so many wars around the world are fuelled by religion, he asked. And why is it that some people are better human beings *before* they become religious (a line that helped to inspire my last book, *How to be a Bad Christian . . . and a Better Human Being*)?

Part of the problem lies in the spirituality of 'sweetness and light', so prevalent these days, which assumes that once we turn to Christ we will live squeaky clean lives free from doubt and reservation, believe the Bible from cover to cover, never have a naughty thought – and wake up every day singing hymns. In other words, the Christian life is all about black and white contrasts and no shades of grey: you either believe in God or you don't, you are either 'saved' or you are a sinner, you are going to heaven when you die or you are bound for hell, the Bible is either literally true or it is a pack of lies. Well, I'm sorry, but that is a million miles from my idea of Christian spirituality.

Reviewing Philip Pullman's book *The Good Man Jesus and the Scoundrel Christ*, Rowan Williams pointed out that Christianity is simple, but never simplistic, that we only get anywhere near the truth when all the easy things to say about God have been deconstructed, so that our image of God ceases to be just a big projection of our own self-centred fantasies. When the dismantling is done, we either sense that we are confronting an energy so immense and unconditioned that we have no words to describe it, or we give up.

Once again, my friend and 'partner in crime' Martin Wroe expresses my feelings perfectly in his poem 'Dark':

You are the dark of the world
When all is brightness and dazzle

You are a deepening mystery
When life is a surfeit of simple solutions

You are the nagging doubt and secret sceptic
When everyone believes so much

You are jangling discord, right out of tune
When all the sounds are harmony

You are abstract art of paint and poem
When our propaganda makes everything clear

You are parched throat, desert defeat
When there's water, water everywhere

You are the silent absence, gone-missing god
When the cacophony of belief is deafening

You are uncharted journey, road less travelled
When we're all mapped-out. Been there, done that

You are stranger in the night, throwing us to the ground
When all we want to do is get away

You are the cloud of unknowing
When we know-it-alls, know it all

You are never ready and take for ever
When we want it now and cannot wait

You are the dark of the world
*When all is brightness and dazzle.**

Faith is a synthesis of belief and doubt. It exists in a constant tension between the two. Belief that is not chastened by honest doubt and questions results in mere certainty, in a fundamentalism which can also lead to a complete loss of faith, or to bigotry and even religious and political radicalism.

It is time to stop seeing darkness as simply the enemy, and embrace it as a potential friend. Though it has often

---

* From Martin Wroe, *How to Lose Your Life* (lulu.com, 2012). The poem is also put to music in Luke Sital-Singh's magnificent song 'Dark'.

been eliminated from Christian spirituality by shallow certainty and hollow triumphalism, darkness has always had an honoured place in the Christian tradition. The expressions 'dark night of the soul' and 'cloud of unknowing' may represent aspects of human experience that are confusing, painful and potentially faith destroying, yet they are also seen to be the necessary path to greater spiritual enlightenment. God is the creator of darkness as well as light.

Religious judgementalism is a particularly ugly thing, which Jesus constantly disparaged. We may not be aware that tearing down others is really a way of bolstering ourselves, yet the underlying thought is something like, 'I would never do that', or 'I could never do such a thing', or 'thank God I am not like that'. We like to have others to condemn in order to reassure ourselves that we could never sink that low. Criticism of others is never simply about the other person, but also an effort to avoid facing one's own faults. When the older brother in the parable of the prodigal son applauds his own righteousness in staying at home and working in his father's fields, it is hard not to conclude that he wished he could have devoured some of his old man's wealth on prostitutes and booze.

Of course, religious judgementalism has nothing to do with real religion. It is simply a 'baptised' expression of the judgementalism that exists within society in general, and which is perhaps part of the 'billy goat' in every one of us. The real point, however, is to acknowledge our own flaws instead of pointing the finger at other people's; to follow the teaching of Jesus by attending to the log in our own eye rather than focusing on the speck in the other person's eye.

At the funeral of the Great Train Robber Bruce Reynolds, the band Alabama 3, in which his son Nick sings and plays harmonica, performed an acoustic version of their evocative song 'Too sick to pray', which contains the line 'Just because I burned my Bible, baby, it don't mean I'm too sick to pray.' There are many people who for all kinds of reasons have 'burned their Bibles', or relinquished the old certainties, who nevertheless reach out to God in some shape or form. And in the pub after Bruce's funeral I had many conversations with such people. One man, who told me he was a former gangster, said, 'I think you've given a lot of people a dilemma here today. The way you talked about God in the service shattered our idea about religion. We're going to have to think again. Maybe one day you'll see me hiding away in the back of one of your services.'

Nick decided he didn't want to go to the crematorium after the funeral service in the church – he didn't want anyone to go. He just found the prospect too upsetting. So I accompanied the coffin with the funeral directors. Once it was laid on the catafalque in the crematorium, just two of us were present for the committal, Lori, the funeral director and a friend of the family, and me.

How strange I thought to be here alone with the remains of this man who masterminded the crime that stunned the nation when I was a young teenager. I don't in any way approve of what he did, but now, being there with all that was left of him in this world, I felt so acutely the sense of his humanity. I felt the excitement of what he had done, and the regret he voiced in his later life. I felt the joys and tears of him, the grief he experienced when he lost his beloved Angie. I said a prayer, and commended him into the hands of the one who came not for the righteous but for sinners like Bruce and me.

I then sent him on his way with his famous catchphrase: 'Be lucky, Bruce.'

14. Finding your spiritual mojo

living and dying with passion

Is life not a thousand times too short for us to bore ourselves?

Friedrich Nietzsche

Pat and I were taking a short holiday at a beautiful woodland caravan park in Nottinghamshire, some years ago. Our daughter Lissy lived nearby so she joined us to walk the dogs in the woods. As we strolled along chatting and enjoying the sunshine and the smell of the pine trees, we noticed a runner approaching on the path behind us, so we took hold of the dogs to keep them out of his way.

As the man in his mid-sixties passed by, he cheerfully greeted us, thanking us for controlling the dogs. Then, after just a hundred yards or so, he drew to a halt and leaned forward with his hands on his knees as if exhausted. The next thing, he fell to the ground and collapsed. I ran to him hastily to offer assistance. The man mumbled incoherently as I bent over him, and was clearly in a lot of trouble. So I ran for help, leaving Pat and Lissy to look after him.

It took me several minutes to get to the site office where the warden telephoned for the paramedics to come, and then joined me in hurriedly returning to where the man was lying. Meanwhile, Lissy placed the man in the recovery position and covered him with her coat. She held him and talked to him, offering him comfort. Then, right there in her arms, he passed away. A moment later the warden arrived and gave him CPR for half an hour until the paramedics finally discovered our remote location. They did everything possible, but the man was long gone.

It turned out that he was a well-known figure in those parts and much loved: a Sunday league football referee, and a dedicated local harrier, who had recovered from triple bypass surgery some years earlier and then become the model of health and fitness.

The whole thing was very upsetting. But if a man is going to die in the arms of a stranger, I cannot think of anyone better to nurse him into eternity than Lissy, our youngest, who is very compassionate and possesses great emotional fortitude.

Afterwards, I managed to find the address of the man's family and wrote to them to let them know what had happened and to say that he was not alone in the woods, but died in loving hands.

I had never before witnessed someone drop dead in front of me like that, and the experience was all the more poignant given that I myself had suffered a heart attack just a few months earlier.

The expression 'heart attack' is a bit like the word 'cancer': people don't like to say it to you directly. Among the many cheering messages I received in the aftermath to my heart attack, only a few mentioned the actual term. Many referred to my 'illness', or spoke of me being 'not well'; one said, we are sorry you have been 'under the weather' lately.

Doctors are more matter of fact about such things. 'You've had a heart attack, Mr Tomlinson', the cardiac consultant told me the morning after I was admitted to hospital. I knew something awful had happened, but it still came as a shock when she said those words. A heart attack was something that other people had, not me. Bear in mind that this was only the second time in my life I had spent a night in a hospital. And the first occasion was for some routine dental surgery. So I wasn't used to doctors telling me unpleasant things about myself. When the doctor left, I lay still in bed but with my mind racing through all the things I still wanted to do with my life, wondering if I would get the chance to do any of them.

Looking back, I feel nothing but gratitude, not just that I survived, but that this event helped me to create such a better quality of life. Over three stone lighter, eating more healthily, and taking regular exercise, I feel fitter, more energetic than I have in years, and younger even.

I recall an occasion just before the heart attack when I ran to catch a bus. It was only a distance of twenty or thirty yards, but I slumped in a heap on the bus thinking, 'I don't think I can do this any more.' It almost felt like a bereavement for a lost stage of my life. Months later, with the heart attack behind me, I decided to skip the bus on my way home from a meeting and run the two-mile journey, which I did with scandalous ease. For some people, surviving a heart attack is an unwelcome detour from 'normal' life; for me, it was the start of a new adventure.

I had known for some years that I needed to make changes to my life, but I kept putting them off. I also slipped into thinking that the changes would require more resolve than I could muster. These were things I thought about mostly in the dead of night when I couldn't sleep, and, by morning, the anxieties generally evaporated, so life continued as before.

After the heart attack, two things became very clear to me. First, that I wanted to become more focused on the things I feel passionate about, and second, that it was absolutely in my power to change my life appropriately. In one of his wonderful blessings, written shortly before he died at the tender age of fifty-three, John O'Donohue beckons us to wake up to the scarcity of our time on earth and to the urgency of becoming free and equal to the call of destiny. Decide carefully, he says, how you can now live the life you would love to look back on from your deathbed.[*]

One of the worst things anyone said to me after the heart attack was, 'At least if you had died, you knew

---

[*] Paraphrased from John O'Donohue, *Benedictus: A Book of Blessings* (Bantam Press, 2007).

where you were going.' It was an innocent, well-meant remark from a neighbour who grew up going to church but kicked the habit years ago. As well as being the sort of thing you might say to a vicar, his words sounded like a mixture of an old mantra from his churchgoing days, and a genuine expression of insecurity about his own eternal destiny.

We don't like to talk about death. It really is the last great taboo. And yet death has such a massive effect on the way we live, especially as we grow older. I'll be honest: I don't want to die. I like living – a lot. When I hear Freddie Mercury singing the Queen song 'Who wants to live forever?' I want to shout out, 'ME! I WANT TO LIVE FOREVER!' And I don't mean, I want to live forever in heaven; I mean, I really, really like this life, here and now, and I want it to go on as long as possible. Yet, actually, the notion of just going on and on, repeating every pleasure and every mistake eternally, would probably turn into hell sooner than I imagine. The fact is, death gives life its passion. It is the urgency that death engenders which drives us from the very depths of our existence. I often look at my beloved dog, Woody, getting older by the day, and wonder what it must be like to not know that you are going to die. That is the difference between me and him: I am driven by goals and aspirations, things I want to achieve; he just keeps on breathing and eating and looking for a squirrel to chase.

In 2011, Jon Underwood was inspired to begin something called the death café in Hackney in East London. He felt that western society had long outsourced discussions about death to doctors, nurses, undertakers and priests. The result, he felt, isn't simply that we don't know how to deal with death, but also that we don't know how to deal with life.

Hosted initially in Jon's home because he couldn't persuade any local café to provide space for a discussion about death, the death café movement was soon born and spread rapidly across Europe, North America and Australasia. As of now, around seven hundred and fifty death cafés have opened since September 2011 – aided by a guide to running a death café produced by Jon and his mum Sue Barsky Reid, who is a psychotherapist. The format of the meetings is simple: a group of people, often strangers, gather to eat cake, drink tea and discuss death.

In an article about the death cafés in the *Guardian* newspaper, Eleanor Tucker writes very positively about her experience of attending one in central Edinburgh. When she left at the end of the evening, she hailed a cab and the chatty driver asked what she had been up to. She hesitated, and then told him. And that was it, they were off, talking about death, to the point that, even after they reached her house, they sat in the taxi for twenty minutes chatting before she went in.

It seems as if people do want to talk about death but not simply in order to deal more openly and satisfactorily with the subject of dying, but in order to get to grips more effectively with the business of living.

My friend Sarah sent me an email recently in which she vented her frustration at the way the church sometimes handles death. 'I have been at a funeral at our church', she wrote, 'when we were told by the minister that most of our life happens when we die . . . something about our life here only being the first page.' Incensed by what she heard, she said she wanted to call out and spoil the funeral and say, 'No, we don't know this. The only life we know about is the one here and now. Let's celebrate the life of the person who has died, instead of going on about what may or may not happen now she's dead.'

I agree with Sarah (though I'm relieved she restrained her emotions and desisted from calling out at the funeral). I share her frustration. I think that funerals where people pretend that the person hasn't really died, just gone to heaven, are deeply infuriating, and inhibit those left behind from properly grieving. The truth is, we don't know what lies beyond this life. Belief may be very powerful and very important to us, but it is not the same as fact. The important thing is to mourn our loss fully and freely, but also to discover afresh what this life is supposed to be about, and live it for all it is worth, leaving God to sort the rest out.

One of the worst aspects of the religious notion of an afterlife is the idea of reward and punishment, which I think distorts the way we look at life here and now. Yes, of course, our actions have consequences, and we must take responsibility for the choices and decisions we make, but I don't think this has anything to do with reward and punishment. And I find the notion of a God who, like some dysfunctional parent, controls us with threats and promises of reward, morally repugnant. This is not a God I can believe in, but a cosmic Santa Claus who keeps lists of which children are naughty and which are good, in order to decide who does or does not deserve gifts.

Surely, if my motivation for living a good Christian life is so that I will get a reward or avoid eternal punishment, I am still trapped in a radical self-centredness from which I need to evolve. A grown-up God for grown-up people is surely one who inspires and energises us to live in this world as passionate and purposeful human beings.

Do I believe in an afterlife? Yes, I do. But I have no idea what that means; moreover, no one I have yet come across has been able to give me a proper explanation of what it means – for the simple reason that, like me, they haven't been there.

I think we need to get away from the reward and punishment, afterlife-driven approach to Christianity, and concentrate on following Jesus of Nazareth in living a passion-filled life; then, eventually, yielding to the passion of death.

The important question is the one posed by John O'Donohue: how can we now live the life we would love to look back on from our deathbed? Sometimes when I take a funeral I begin with a prayer that thanks God for a life 'well lived'. It's a prayer I find myself hoping that I myself can live up to.

The most basic thing about a life well lived is for it to be authentic, by which I mean, lived from a real place within. Far too many of us live a life that is expected of us, rather than the life that is truly ours. Even when we try to internalise the ideals of our heroes, this too can be a way of avoiding discovering who we truly are and what it is that we believe in. I am not expected to be Gandhi or Martin Luther King; I am expected to be Dave Tomlinson, that is all.

I find that people get very confused by the idea of 'vocation'. We often think of a vocation or a calling as something for the chosen few, especially for priests or nuns, or people with a special sense of mission in life, or people in certain professions like a doctor or a teacher. The rest of us just make our way in life, doing what we fancy or what works out but without any special sense of vocation. And very often, the notion of being 'called' is based on the old picture of an external God 'out there', a 'man upstairs' sort of God who interrupts the normal processes of life to speak to us in some special or super-natural way.

The truth is that the real 'voice' is within, embedded in who we are. And the way that we hear it is to follow the old Quaker maxim that says, 'Let your life speak.' In other words, 'Discover the beliefs and values that come from a mature and grounded place within you, and let them guide you.'

Part of this process, of course, lies in knowing what it is that you believe in – not the hand-me-down rules or doctrines you have inherited from parents, teachers or church, but the truths that resonate deep down. The Quakers call it the 'inner light' or 'that of God' in every-one. The monk Thomas Merton calls it true self. Humanists may see it as identity and integrity. However we name it, it is about finding your own bedrock, for this is where God, the Ground of our Being, resides.

Finding our bedrock and working out what this means for our life in terms of particular activities and projects is not an evening's work. It emerges little by little on a life journey. However, without unearthing what it is that we truly believe in, we carry around baggage that is not our own: baggage that stops our true life from speaking.

One of my favourite writers and poets, May Sarton, reflecting on her life says, 'Now I become myself. It's taken time, many years and places. I have been dissolved and shaken, worn other people's faces . . .'[*] It can take a long time to become the person you have always been deep down. Like a child dressing up, we go through phases, long or short, of trying on other people's 'clothes' before discovering what really fits us.

The Quaker Parker Palmer relates how when his daughter and her new-born baby came to live with him, he watched his granddaughter from her earliest days, and realised something that had eluded him when his own children were small. He recognised that she arrived in the world as *this* kind of person rather than *that*, or *that*, or *that*. She did not show up simply as raw material to be

---

[*] May Sarton, *Collected Poems* (Norton, 1974).

shaped by the world, but with her own gifted form, with the shape of her own sacred soul.[*]

Jesus famously said, 'Unless you become like children you will never enter the kingdom of God.'[†] The thing I love about children is their openness to life; their receptivity towards people, towards situations, towards the life force, which is God's Spirit within. And it is in childhood that vocation is revealed and formed: witnessed in the inclinations and proclivities that were planted from birth, in our likes and dislikes, in the things that attract or repel us, in the way we move and do things and relate to others.

As Parker Palmer says, we arrive in the world with birthright gifts – then we spend the first half of our lives abandoning or letting others disabuse us of them. If we manage eventually to wake up to admit to our loss, we may then spend the second half of life trying to recover and reclaim the gift we once possessed.

Some of us are very happy with our lives; we have discovered to some extent who we are, and have found ways to express this. Others of us feel frustrated because we live under the burden of wearing other people's 'clothes' – roles and responsibilities that either don't fit or weigh too heavily upon us. Or we live with a 'dark cloud'

---

[*] Parker J. Palmer, *Let Your Life Speak* (Jossey-Bass, 2000).
[†] Matthew 18:3.

of voices that buffet and undermine our self-worth and confidence. For some, life feels like a giant jigsaw where key pieces are missing, so it never quite comes together.

I recently chatted with a hugely successful woman, who many people admire or envy. She had heard me giving a *Pause for Thought* early one morning on BBC Radio 2, where I spoke about the voice of the inner critic that relentlessly undermines some people's self-confidence. 'Mine is the voice of my father,' she said.

'Surely, your father must be very proud of you?' I enquired.

'No, he thinks I've wasted my life,' she said. 'So far as he is concerned, I should have been a successful academic.'

Despite her massive achievements, and the fact that she had clearly followed her passion, he disapproved. And she was left with his niggling voice inside.

Writing to the church at Rome, Paul intimates that our truest expression of divine worship is to present all that we are to the service of God in the world – to find our passion and pursue it. Don't be pressed into the mould that the world wants to fit you into, but allow your mind-set to be renewed by God's Spirit within you so that you can find your mojo (my expression rather than St Paul's) – discover who and what you are deep down.

Our deepest calling is to discover our authentic self and

to grow into that, regardless of whether it fits some image of who we think we ought to be. As we do this we will not only discover meaning to our life, we will also find a pathway into effective service to the world. As Frederick Buechner comments,[*] vocation is where our deep gladness and the world's deep need intersect.

* *Wishful Thinking*, HarperCollins, 1993.

15. The alchemy of community

transforming spiritual networks

I also believe that it's almost impossible for people to change alone. We need to join with others who will push us in our thinking and challenge us to do things we didn't believe ourselves capable of.

Frances Moore Lappé

Judi's life changed when a boy attacked her in one of her classes as a supply teacher. A girl said something nasty about the boy's family and he went for her. He was only eight, but seemed intent on killing the girl. As Judi tried to intervene, he sent her flying. She hit her head on the table, fell on her back, and passed out. When she came to, everywhere was silent. She says it was the quietest classroom she had ever known.

The attack and the back pain she still experiences as a result are part of a sequence of events through which Judi's health inexorably declined. Her father, a great support to her, died suddenly. An intimidating ex-prisoner moved into a flat in her house. Arthritis began to assert itself. And she was mugged twice near to her home.

Previously, Judi had been the person to intervene in disputes – she remembers stopping two men on a train from stubbing cigarette butts out on another man – but now she was withdrawing. She was changing as a person. She became increasingly afraid and unhappy, and more and more unwell until she got to the stage where she couldn't go outside. She became focused on protecting herself so went into isolation.

While attending a Christian hospital for help with her fatigue and burnout, a friend told Judi that she should find a church. That was when she turned up at St Luke's, which happened to be on the next street to where she lived.

Judi says that becoming part of St Luke's played a massive part in her slowly recovering her health and confidence – being in the place, day in day out, to meet with a small group to say morning prayers. With the reassurance of a loving community, and also the help of a form of self-hypnosis called Autogenic Therapy, Judi says she is a different person now.[*]

Thirty-eight years ago, she gave birth to a son, who in the circumstances she felt forced to give up for adoption. It was a heart-breaking decision, but felt like the only thing she could do. For thirty-five years she had no contact with him and knew nothing about what his life had become. It often made her weepy, especially around the anniversary of his birthday.

Then, out of the blue, the wonderful woman who adopted Jon contacted Judi to tell her what a fine man her son had turned out to be, and that he was recently married and would like to meet her. Judi was overjoyed. And to cut a long story short, Pat and I accompanied her to meet Jonathan and his family. It was a long journey with plenty of time for reflection; Judi wondered how it would go. Finally we arrived, and I shall never forget that moment of meeting, especially the look on Judi's face when a warm-hearted, handsome man took her in his

---

[*] Judi's story is told in Martin Wroe, *The Gospel According to Everyone* (lulu.com, 2011), which contains twelve stories of people in the St Luke's community.

arms for the first time. My job turns up some mighty wonderful occasions, but they really don't get any better than this.

After lunch with Jon's marvellous parents and his new wife, we prepared to depart for London. Jon announced that he had a gift for Judi. Standing next to his wife, he pulled from his pocket an ultrasound photograph of their unborn child, Judi's grandchild, who she knew nothing about until then. She was gobsmacked! Never in her wildest dreams did she think she would be a grandmother. Jon's mum also presented Judi with a photo album of him over the years.

The following week, she proudly shared her photo album with the other family that she has discovered, the family of St Luke's where she is loved and respected. 'I suppose I've lived a messy life,' Judi says, 'but the cross of Jesus is quite messy and it is the church which mistakenly tries to sanitise it. From the messy life I've found inner understanding, compassion and humility. Living on benefits can mean you face financial poverty, but I feel very rich as part of this church.'

Judi's life is changed out of all recognition. From being a withdrawn person when I first met her, holed up in the safety of her home, she has become a source of inspiration and support to many, contributing energetically to the life of St Luke's and also the wider community.

I could tell many other stories quite different to Judi's, yet strangely alike, of lives transformed through the alchemy of community. Often, these communities will be specifically Christian, like St Luke's, but not always. The Spirit of Christ is not limited to working exclusively through Christian people or church groups. Indeed, frankly, Jesus is sometimes channelled more powerfully and effectively through people and groups that are not Christian, or in any way religious.

Yet the church exists to be a sacrament, a flesh-and-blood communication of who Jesus is and what he represents. In one of his letters in the New Testament, Paul likens the church to the body of Christ: his arms and legs, his ears and eyes and heart in the world. The church's mission is not merely to fill pews, or to build more or bigger churches, but to be the presence of Christ in the world, an effective expression of divine love and grace.

Another volume would need to be written for me to describe the church as I envisage it, so I will settle for pinpointing four things that rate high on my list of priorities for St Luke's as we attempt to express the Spirit of Jesus Christ.

1. Inclusion
In the Gospels, especially Luke's Gospel, Jesus is portrayed as a figure of radical inclusion. He welcomed and affirmed

women and children at a time when they were invisible and devoid of social status, he treated reviled Samaritans as friends and equals, he responded to the cries of those on the fringes, he healed the servant of a despised Roman soldier, and embraced the tax collectors who were seen as collaborators with the Romans, he ate and drank with prostitutes, publicans and sinners, and was charged with being their friend. In the end, his inclusive practices got him into deep water: he was crucified, literally, for eating with the wrong people.

Undoubtedly, there are many churches that embody Christ's inclusive spirit, yet far too many people still find the church unwelcoming. Before finding St Luke's, many of my lesbian and gay friends pretty much gave up hope of discovering a place of acceptance in the church.

But it is not just gay people who feel excluded. Many people whose lives are seen by the church to be 'messy' experience rejection. One couple who asked me to marry them had tried four other churches before coming to me. At each one they were rejected because they had previous marriages in which one of them was deemed to be the 'guilty' party. Sometimes people experience an initial welcome but soon discover that they need to 'clean up' in order to be fully accepted. Another couple living together but not married were refused communion in one church. Little wonder some people don't hang around for long.

I find it very sad that the Eucharist, which I see as a central symbol of divine inclusion, can become a symbol of rejection to many. It is the point in lots of services where the church becomes an exclusive club, and the uninitiated 'sit there like a lemon – or a grubby outsider', as one man put it to me.

At St Luke's, following the example of Jesus who ate and drank with whoever joined him around the table, we offer bread and wine to every single person, without exception. Everyone who holds out his or her hand to receive will have it filled. For me, the Eucharist is a gospel act – an invitation to receive God's unconditional love – where everyone is included, and no one turned away. I know people whose faith journey began through eating bread and wine – not simply in the receiving of communion but at a church lunch after the service, or through a meal in someone's home, or during a party. All of these too may become Eucharistic occasions.

'St Luke's is the only church (or place come to think of it) that I have encountered full and unconditional inclusiveness,' one person wrote to me, 'a hard act to follow.' I don't know if everyone who turns up at St Luke's feels quite so welcome, but this is certainly our aspiration, not because we are nice people, but because radical inclusion is utterly fundamental to what Jesus is about.

2. Truth

By 'truth' I am not talking about doctrines and dogma. I see truth as more of a conversation than a statement or a creed. To be a community of truth means to create the space for an ongoing discussion about things that matter – conducted with passion, but also mutual respect. A community of truth is a place where there is freedom of conscience and conviction, where acceptance is not based on believing the 'right' things, but on becoming part of the conversation; where there is debate and argument, and civil disagreement, but also love.

As I have travelled around this country and abroad, I have repeatedly found people, religious and non-religious, who are looking for truthful conversation about things that matter. 'Where can I find deep conversations?' a man asked me in a pub in Liverpool. I would love to have said, 'Go to your local church' – and who knows, maybe he would have found them there, but equally, it may have been the last place to find them.

In 1990, along with a few other people, I started Holy Joes, a group in a pub in South London where people could engage in the sort of deep conversation about faith, doubt and religion that they couldn't find in church. Every Tuesday night for ten years we hosted the kind of honest debate that proved to be the salvation of many a person's faith. More recently, in the spirit of Holy Joes, we have launched 'Public House' in a bar very close to St Luke's to provide a similar space for 'bad Christian back-chat'. I think that lots of people want the conversation, but will not come to church to find it.

Ten years of running Holy Joes, where many hundreds, perhaps thousands, of people passed through, convinced me that the church needs to host debate – deep conversa-tions. But it is vital that 'deep conversation' is not simply code for 'we want to convert you'. Once we place our hand on the wheel to try to guide the conversation down a particular track, it ceases to be a conversation and becomes a mere sales pitch.

In my experience, truthful conversation always leads back to things that really matter – to things of ultimate concern – regardless of the topic on offer.

When a man came to hear me speak in a pub recently, he stood up during the question time and said, 'I came here as an atheist, and I leave as an atheist. But bizarrely, I believe everything this man has said tonight.' Beyond any particularities of the conversation, the thing that united us was a sense of accountability to something beyond ourselves, a transcendent reality which he called 'truth' and I call 'God'.

Ultimately, truth isn't something to reduce to a set of

words, despite our constant efforts to do so, but something to be lived. The hallmark of a community of truth is a commitment to live truthfully, i.e. from a sense of integrity and ultimate concern. Jesus did not say, 'believe these three or four things and you will have eternal life'. He said, 'I *am* the way and the truth and the life – follow me.'

3. Ritual

The word 'ritual' is often used in a negative sense for something that is merely routine and lifeless. But good ritual is in itself a form of alchemy, a dramatic enactment that can bring about change or transformation in the participants, or the situation.

In preparing events and services at St Luke's, we are constantly looking for simple symbolic actions that can help us to connect with God in our lives in fresh ways. I try especially hard to do this when the church is packed with non-churchgoers. One effective piece of ritual can achieve what a thousand words will never accomplish.

So, for example, if I have fifty or a hundred non-church-going people attending a christening, I will almost certainly be faced with a defiantly passive congregation – until I introduce the ritual of 'prayer stones'.

After splashing water on the baby, I invite the congre-gation to offer a prayer for the child. I explain that a prayer is just like a wish, and then invite them to come forward and drop a stone in the water, first pausing with it in their hand to find their 'wish' for the child's life. The response is always overwhelming. Everyone takes part. Many times people will say that it was the highlight of the service for them. And now I have parents specifically asking if they can have 'stone prayers' as part of their child's christening. One woman told me, 'If prayer is as simple as that, I'm going to do it more often.'

Holy Week and Easter offer plenty of opportunity for ritual moments. This year at St Luke's we were blessed to have as a main focus a beautiful, large painting by Jake Lever called *The Blue, and the Dim, and the Gold*. The painting features a lone figure in a small vessel, pausing for a moment on a dark lake. The boat is dwarfed by a vast landscape containing chaotic splashes of dark colour in the hillside, while above there is a gilded sky, created from gold leaf that reflects in the ripples on the lake. Jake describes the painting as a meditation on the universal human experience of weakness, uncertainty and vulnerability.

On Good Friday, the painting stood in the chancel. There were also various 'stations' around the church with small golden boats made by Jake where people could interact with the Good Friday theme in the context of their own suffering and hope. Stones were dropped into

231

the font – this time to symbolise various kinds of loss in our lives. Candles were lit for those who are suffering in our world today. And prayers were written and placed into a boat in front of the painting. We even made our own boats from a template provided by Jake as a symbol of hope for our journey.

Together with Jake's magnificent piece of art, these ritual moments worked magic in our lives, enabling us to catch the spirit of Good Friday in unique ways. Afterwards, one person reflected that the whole thing 'drew us through the Good Friday story and theme of suffering, surrender, sacrifice and death into a spiritual exercise of reflecting, mourning and yielding, which left me and I'm sure many others feeling nourished and healed'.

4. Empowerment

Healthy community enables people to discover their potential. I love groups like Centre 404, the charity housed just across the road from where I live, which empowers people with severe disabilities to achieve things they never could achieve alone. Yet we all need the alchemy of community in order to comprehend, and move towards, our greater potential.

The idea that in order to grow and prosper, churches require strong top-down leadership centred around a single vision for the community is completely wrong in my view. What we actually need is for the church to be a fellowship of emancipation and enabling, with leadership focused on releasing and facilitating rather than directing and managing. Our goal should not be to have large congregations passively admiring the talents of a few, but active communities where there is freedom of imagination, initiative and responsibility.

Our final ritual at the end of a Sunday morning service at St Luke's is 'the notices'. Frankly, it sometimes takes too long, yet it often provides an amazing mirror on our community. This was highlighted to me when a visiting church minister on sabbatical from his church in Switzerland seemed to find 'the notices' the most challenging and inspiring part of the entire service.

That morning there were notices about the sale of fairly traded goods after the service, an invitation to sing that afternoon in a home for people with dementia, a request for Christmas gifts for the children of prisoners in Holloway Prison, a request for food donations to the food bank, an invitation for newcomers to join a pub group where they could get to know people in the church, and an appeal for volunteers for the homeless night shelter in the church which was about to begin. The visiting minister was flabbergasted to discover that these were overwhelmingly the initiatives of individuals in the church without any central organisation. 'If such things were to happen in my church, I would need to make them happen,' he told me afterwards.

Actually, these were just the tip of the iceberg in terms of the exciting projects and events organised by people in St Luke's. We see it as our job to provide the space, and to support people in using their own imagination and initiative in making things happen, and not to control, or manage, or direct them.

I can't guarantee that you will find a church community like this at the end of your road. But perhaps your local church would value you trying to help it become more like it.

However, there is a greater vision; the alchemy of community is not limited to churches or religious establishments. Anyone can begin a group in a pub, or a front room, to set up deep conversations and see where it leads. Or there may be groups already in existence that you can join – a philosophy club in a local pub, a 'death café', or some other group that organises talks or discussions about things that matter. I want to do everything I can to nurture and cultivate deep conversations – in churches, pubs, living rooms, coffee shops: networks of transformation.

The real point is that, while you can be a bad Christian all on your own, it is much better to share the journey with others, to activate a network of fellow travellers, to benefit from the alchemy of kindred spirits.

I leave you with Bobby Baker, an incredibly talented performance artist, and a dear friend, who journeyed for several years through and out of serious mental illness and speaks of the magic of community in her process of healing:

Ultimately I have got better because of a wealth of fragments washed in over the deepest reefs of family love – assorted dazzling scraps of wisdom, knowledge and experience; brilliant phrases and images; tiny golden acts of kindness and care; friendship, laughter and sparkling wit – which have gradually heaped my mind full of treasure. These are riches to comfort me and fill my mind with the miraculous joy of being alive, and make me happier (most of the time) than I ever dreamed it was possible to be.*

---

* Bobby Baker, *Daily Drawings: Mental Illness and Me* (Profile Books, 2008).

16. The bad Christian's manifesto

- To follow the way of Jesus rather than rules and conventions.
- To doubt and question WITHOUT fear, and never be daunted by orthodoxies and authority figures.
- To make a priority of kindness and compassion, and pursue justice for all people.
- To embrace messiness and imperfection while aspiring to be all that we can be.
- To live courageously, and resist being motivated by guilt or fear.

The Bad Christian's Manifesto

- To love the world and honour it as God's body.
- To have parties, laugh often, enjoy friends and welcome strangers.
- To resist passing judgement, and befriend people in the margins.
- To look for God in every person and situation.

Acknowledgements

Writing doesn't come naturally to me. It's too solitary an affair. And it's hard work. So I am very distractible – another cup of coffee, someone I need to see, another check on my emails. When I was struggling to finish one particular chapter I found myself magnificently distracted by an email from Amazon inviting me, ironically, to pre-order the finished product. Naturally, I took it as an omen and went ahead and ordered the book. My only regret being that there was no 'look inside' facility to check out the chapter I was struggling to write.

The truth is, a book is never the product of a solitary individual, a lone author, but a whole community. So here goes.

Thanks to Rob Pepper, my friend and visual collaborator, for marrying my words to beautiful drawings while at the same time rebuilding his house, and to Katherine Venn, another friend who is also my editor, whose input and encouragement – and promise of a whisky when I handed in the final draft – helped to get me across the line. Thanks to the awesome Hodder Faith team for transforming my vision into glorious reality. Thanks also to my friend and colleague Martin Wroe for his lateral inspiration and wonderful poems. Thanks to everyone who let me tell their stories, and to the people of St Luke's who provide me with the best job in the world. Huge thanks to my readers – people I may never meet yet who constantly live in my mind and heart as I sit in front of my laptop.

Thanks to family and friends who believe in me and help to make me who I am. But most of all, thanks to my wife and dearest friend Pat, who has lived patiently and good-naturedly with the grumpiness and frustration that often accompanies my writing. She vastly reduced my workload when I needed it, made me laugh, and showed me what a better human being looks like.

Appendix
Sermon to The Sunday Assembly

The power of stories, myths and metaphors as ways of seeing the world. And why humans have enjoyed the Easter tale.

Okay, let's get the disclaimer out of the way. I am not an atheist!

I am a vicar, actually.

But Sanderson Jones and Pippa Evans are my friends. And I am a fan of what is going on here at the Sunday Assembly. Indeed, so much so that I am now widely cited as the vicar who gives approval to the Sunday Assembly, which has resulted in me receiving some wonderfully 'loving' emails from brothers and sisters around the world, telling me that I have shamed the church and the name of God. I am, as you can tell, a pretty *bad* Christian. But I am a Christian all the same.

That said, I confess I frequently cringe at being connected with the 'C' word. I cringe at the stupidity of some of the things preached in Christ's name. I cringe at the way some

Christians behave. I cringe at quite a lot of church history. I cringe at some parts of the Bible. I want to scream at the top of my voice in holy anger at the homophobia, sexism and other forms of prejudice pedalled by some Christians. If I thought that any of these things had anything to do with Jesus Christ or what he represents, I would be off like a shot! But I don't think that.

Often, when people want to determine whether I'm a real Christian or just a dodgy liberal (and usually they have already made up their mind on the matter) they ask me one of those knockout questions: Do I believe in the *bodily* resurrection of Jesus, or the virgin birth?

I have no problem discussing these matters; I wrote a book called *Re-Enchanting Christianity* which offers my views on these and many other things. But the problem is that, mostly, the questions are predicated on the assumption that we have to be one kind of literalist or another: either a religious literalist who equates truth with fact, or a scientific literalist who also equates truth with fact but from the reverse perspective.

The religious literalist says if the story isn't factual it *can't* be true; the scientific literalist argues that *since* religious stories *aren't* factual, therefore they cannot be true. I am not a literalist of either variety. I dislike all kinds of fundamentalism – religious and atheist. But I do believe there is something called truth, which is ultimately greater than literal descriptions could ever encapsulate or express.

Stories can be perfectly truthful without being factual. If you read novels, watch films, or appreciate art, you know what I'm talking about. A story like *The Life of Pi*, for example, can be profoundly truthful without being a literal account of something that happened. Indeed, that is what *The Life of Pi* is all about. Also, a portrayal of a real life event can sometimes be more truthfully narrated or portrayed in a picture from an artist's imagination than, say, a photograph or a factual description. I have shelves of books of poetry that are packed with wonderful, liberating, life-enhancing truth without saying anything that is necessarily factual.

The so-called 'parable' of the Good Samaritan in the New Testament is an interesting example. I say 'so-called' because actually neither Jesus, nor Luke who wrote the gospel, says it is a parable. Jesus introduces the story, simply saying, 'A man went down from Jerusalem to Jericho . . .' Well, did a man go down from Jerusalem to Jericho or not? Was the man real or just a figment of Jesus' imagination? Is the story fact or fiction? Much more importantly, what the heck does it matter? The better question is: in what way does the story speak to us?

What does it tell us about the world, about our fellow human beings, about social behaviour, about religion, about me?

A Native American storyteller always begins telling his tribe's story of creation by saying: 'Now I don't know if it happened this way or not, but I know this story is true.' In other words, the story is a source of wisdom – truth to his people; it conveys important things about the world and how they should live in it. But it's not literally true.

We all love Aesop's *Fables*; the stories aren't factual – the north wind and the sun didn't really have an argument . . . did they? But the stories are true all the same. We human beings find truth much more palatable, more persuasive, more entertaining and therefore more powerful in story form, or in a picture or a film than as a rational proposition.

Literalism (religious and non-religious) cripples the imagination because it cannot fathom that something could be true on one level and not on another. A world without myth and metaphor and sacred (or deeply respected) story, where everything is reduced to fact and mathematical equation or rational statement is a bleak place where I would not wish to live.

Nowadays, the word 'myth' has become synonymous with 'untrue'. But properly speaking this isn't what myth means. Technically, a myth is a hermeneutical device – a way of interpreting truths about the world and of human experience in narrative form.

A myth is a lens, a window on life. It's not about giving you a pile of creedal statements to recite and believe in – I think Christians have got it wrong when they present faith as a list of doctrinal boxes we're supposed to tick. To me, Christianity is a spiritual practice, a way of approaching life, based on the life and teachings of Jesus. It's not about believing five incredible things before you've finished eating your first chocolate egg on Easter morning! It's a way of being.

I'm a campfire kind of person myself (better still, a dining table type), who likes the idea of passionate conversations round the fire or over a bottle of wine or two after dinner, chewing over the meaning of the story. A myth is more of a point of engagement than a dogma.

What literalism misses completely is the dimension of mystery or wonder. Yes, I know that 'mystery' can be an intellectual cop-out, but some things – like love, for example – are mysterious and much better talked about poetically rather than placed in a test tube. Not everything can be categorised as fact or fiction.

So why is the Easter story so compelling regardless of our religious inclinations? For a similar reason that

Shawshank Redemption is one of the most popular films of all time – because Easter is about hope and redemption, rebirth and new possibility. It says 'Have a little faith, a little forgiveness, a little hope that things can be different.'

Isn't it interesting that (in the northern hemisphere, at least, where the story originates), Easter occurs in the spring? I think religion works best when it interacts with nature and the seasons. Autumn and winter introduce death and decay as part of the cycle of life. In a lovely piece entitled 'A Winter Psalm of Fearlessness', which I often read at funerals, the priest and writer Edward Hays says:

> *I am surrounded by a peaceful ebbing,*
> *as creation bows to the mystery of life;*
> *all that grows and lives must give up life,*
> *yet it does not really die.*
>
> *As plants surrender their life,*
> *bending, brown and wrinkled,*
> *and yellow leaves of trees*
> *float to the lawn like parachute troops,*
> *they do so in a sea of serenity.*

Yet the deeper story in nature and Easter is one of hope. There is death, but there is also resurrection, rebirth, a new start. Human life, along with the rest of nature, passes through a constant cycle. Not just Easter but the whole Christian calendar is a way of narrating / interpreting this pattern of existence within a faith tradition. We need stories – lenses through which to view our life on earth – whether they are religious or not. I guess this is the great appeal of paganism, which has gone through something of a revival in recent decades: it attempts to reconnect people to nature, to the life force within nature

When I grow weary of religion and fancy walking away, it's the story of Jesus that brings me back. It is a tale of a powerless peasant who stood up against the authorities, who became a voice for ordinary people and gave corrupt religious leaders a hard time. It's about someone who went about doing good and showing compassion to ordinary people; who was accused of being a glutton and a drunkard because he loved eating and drinking with the wrong type of people; who brought hope to the masses.

In the end, the threat was too great, so crooked politicians and religious leaders plotted to have him killed. But even in death he triumphed over malicious self-interest by not succumbing to hatred and vengeance. And his spirit lives on in the hearts of many who follow the same way.

I happen to believe this story really occurred, but even if I didn't I would still believe it was true.

And the world is full of Christ figures who are not necessarily religious, whose stories go on. Nelson Mandela is an obvious example. For 27 long years, during his imprisonment, his life was on hold – or was it? Like a seed buried in the hard, cold earth waiting for warmer days, Mandela nurtured hope and practiced resurrection. Then, on a day that none of us who saw can ever forget, he strode out of Victor Verster prison in Cape Town. Every step was an expression of resurrection in practice. He later said, 'As I walked out the door toward the gate that would lead to my freedom, I knew if I didn't leave my bitterness and hatred behind, I'd still be in prison.' There was death, but there was also resurrection.

Philip Pulman – a master storyteller says:

'After nourishment, shelter and companionship, stories are the thing we need most in the world.'

Amen to that! But the stories need to be redemptive in some way. And that is why the Easter story is so important to me and to millions of others: it is a story of hope and redemption in the face of hatred and injustice.

Do you wish this wasn't the end?
Are you hungry for more great teaching, inspiring
testimonies, ideas to challenge your faith?

Join us at www.hodderfaith.com, follow us on Twitter
or find us on Facebook to make sure you get the latest from
your favourite authors.

Including interviews, videos, articles, competitions
and opportunities to tell us just what you thought about
our latest releases.

www.hodderfaith.com

 HodderFaith

 @HodderFaith

 HodderFaithVideo

HODDER
WHERE FAITH IS INSPIRED